Applying LEAN PROJECT MANAGEMENT

Combining Lean Tools with Project Management To Outpace Competitors and Increase Profits

L. T. Harland, PMP

PM Trailblazer, LLC

PM Trailblazer, LLC

www.PMtrailblazer.com

Hudson, Ohio

Copyright 2020 by L.T. Harland, PMP

Front cover photography: Margie Seibert

www.MargieDesign.com

ISBN: 978-0-578-72799-8

PM Trailblazer, LLC

Dedication

In memory of my dad, Kenny Harland,
who rolled up his sleeves to help anyone (including me)
solve just about any kind of problem.

Contents

Introduction

Hello, my name is L. T. Harland. I have been managing projects and developing new products for over thirty years — long enough to have experienced many successes, intermingled with some embarrassing mistakes here and there. But the mistakes are what helped me learn the most. Through both the successes and the mistakes, I learned how to manage projects faster and smarter by removing wasted effort and by delivering what customers valued. In other words, I learned how to practice Lean Project Management. I also worked with hundreds of other people who have managed projects and products, so I've seen many of their successes and mistakes.

The story in this book is based on collective good and bad experiences, with hopes that you'll learn from both and avoid making the same mistakes that I and others have made.

STARTING OUT

I began my career in the toy industry in the mid 1980's as a young design engineer. While I was engineering new products, I was also expected to *manage* them. Managing projects and products involved ensuring the design, engineering, manufacturing, testing and delivery to the customer were all completed on time, with the promised features, and within a given cost limit. It also involved working closely with marketing product managers whose job was to create a Business Plan, to determine what new products people would want to buy, to determine the selling price, and to develop an advertising plan.

Back in the 1980's, the toy industry was booming. The projects I managed involved the creation of new products that were manufactured and sold around the world. The company I worked for was in a race with our competitors to deliver the next big concept to our customers (mostly large retailers), consumers (parents and grandparents) and end users (babies, toddlers, and older children) as soon as possible. Doing that required a team of people to come up with ideas and turn them into products that would be available on store shelves in less than a year. We didn't follow project management principles or product development processes. We didn't even know those things existed. We were just trying to create products and get them on the store shelves as quickly as possible.

Most of those projects and products were completed with success. In fact, I still see some of them today in homes, yards, day care centers, churches, public playgrounds, doctor's offices, airport play areas, and even hotels.

But some projects were real fiascos that would make good case studies on how not to execute projects. Some products never made it to the store shelves. Others made it but were seriously behind schedule or introduced at higher than expected costs – which meant lower than expected profit margins. Some provided less value than customers were expecting. Some caused internal "fire drills." In those cases, team members from other projects and departments had to be urgently borrowed to work on my projects to get them back on track. Every project and product meant a great deal to me and I wanted them all to be successful, so when any of them didn't go well it was a very stressful time. None of my projects back then followed Lean principles. I did the best I could with what I knew at the time.

Of the products I created that are still being manufactured today, I assume they continue to earn profits, twenty to thirty years after they originally entered the market. But how much *more* profit would they have earned, over time, if those products had been delivered earlier, at a lower cost, with better quality or with greater value to the customer?

I sometimes calculate things like this: *if just one of those products had been introduced at just $.25 less cost, and 300,000 units of that product were sold annually over the last twenty years, well that's $1,500,000 in additional profits!* And that's the lost earnings on just one of hundreds of products at just one company! Imagine all the products we know of that could have been introduced at a lower cost, introduced on time or earlier, or made with a greater level of quality and value. If we could have avoided project management mis-haps, imagine all the struggles and stresses we could have saved ourselves, not to mention all the profits we left on the table! Those un-earned profits could have been re-invested back into the company for increased research funding, better technology, more resources, increased paychecks or greater retirement benefits.

TWENTY YEARS LATER

After my toy industry adventure, I wanted to do something completely different, so I joined the aircraft industry. My job was to lead the development of high-tech products for private and commercial airplanes, helicopters, and business jets. I was relieved to discover that the company I worked for took project management very seriously. Think about it. When you're on an airplane that's thirty thousand feet in the air, you want to know that the people who created that airplane took meticulous care during each and every step of the plane's development, including conducting thorough risk assessments.

Within my first thirty days at that company, I attended a basic project management class. Initially I was irritated when my boss asked me to take the class. After all, in my previous work life I led a global group of more than sixty people in project management and product development, and I didn't have to attend any training to do it.

But during the first day of class I learned the proper terminology for the steps I had been taking over the past twenty years. I also learned key steps I had *not* been taking but should have, and I discovered the root causes of why some of my previous projects had failed. And that was just the first day!

I was on fire with wanting to learn more about project management. After that class, I attended an advanced class, and then went on to take more related classes. I studied during evenings and weekends for the Project Management Professional (PMP)® exam and earned my certificate as a Project Management Professional.

After my aircraft industry experience, I worked in the automotive and healthcare industries, leading manufacturing projects, software launches, software upgrades and more. I created project management and other curriculums and enjoyed teaching and coaching over a thousand people in several countries.

PM TRAILBLAZER, LLC

I love helping people reach their goals, so in 2016 I started PM Trailblazer, LLC. PM Trailblazer provides project management, product development, and many other types of customized coaching and training. We have helped government, public and private organizations of all sizes and in many different industries.

It was through PM Trailblazer and working with our clients that I began to appreciate Lean techniques. I started thinking about how applying Lean principles could streamline project management.

For more information about Lean Project Management and to download free project management templates, visit www.PMtrailbazer.com.

HOW I CAN HELP YOU

Valuable lessons I've learned from my own experiences and from observing other organizations are summarized within the story in this book. While reading it you will learn over twenty Lean Project Management techniques, when to use them, and how to apply them. These skills will help you to manage your projects more efficiently, satisfy your customers, reduce stress, and meet schedule, cost, and performance goals. Applying the techniques in this book will help you to outpace your competitors and increase profits.

About This Book

TODAY'S SITUATION

Organizations tend to send their people to either Lean training or to project management training, but rarely to both. Lean training focuses on adding value and removing waste, while project management focuses on meeting objectives by leading a project from start to finish.

Project management and Lean methodologies complement each other extraordinarily well. Why? Good project managers apply their skills to deliver projects on time, within cost targets and at the expected performance levels. They understand the life cycle of a project. They know where to start and how to document things like project deliverables, acceptance criteria, changes to the project's scope and lessons learned. They know how to manage costs, schedules, deadlines, resources, stakeholders, risks, issues, communications, status updates, and even internal politics — and they deliver what's promised.

Applying Lean techniques can enable organizations to give their customers the value they expect, resulting in happy, repeat customers. Having happy and repeat customers leads to increased profits. Applying Lean methods can also enable organizations to reduce or eliminate wasted time and wasted money, again resulting in increased profits.

I've talked with many Lean experts who have struggled with managing projects. They didn't know how to set up a project with a solid foundation. I've also seen many project managers go through all the proper steps of managing projects while wasting significant amounts of time and money on work that didn't provide the value the customer or the end user expected.

We need to have Lean techniques and project management skills working together.

WE CAN'T AFFORD NOT TO PRACTICE LEAN PROJECT MANAGEMENT

Some people say that applying project management methods takes too long. They say it's not worth the effort, and they don't have time for it. They just want to get a project started and get it done.

But even in organizations with a high level of project management maturity, only about sixty to seventy percent of projects are completed on time, meet their committed cost targets, and meet their intended business goals. So we must change *how* we manage projects.

When we skip over basic project management steps, and a project veers off track, as so many do, leaders then cave in and agree that extra time should be taken to go back and plan correctly in order to get the project back on track again. That's so wasteful!

By then, commitments have been missed. Internal and external customers are upset. People (likely the project manager) may have been removed from the project — or the company — for not meeting the project's goals.

To improve those dreadful statistics and achieve project success, we need to practice solid project management. There are many steps involved in good project management, so to be efficient we need to manage projects in the Leanest ways possible.

HOW TO QUICKLY GET RESULTS FROM THIS BOOK

Section 1: The Flying Machine, Inc.

Read this section to get the foundation of the story, which starts by describing how a high-tech company called The Flying Machine, Inc. experienced a significant project failure. To help understand what happened and to position the company for future success, the CEO hires a Lean Project Management expert, Sam Lazarus.

After leading some learning sessions in both project management and Lean methods, Sam coaches a team through the Lean execution of a large project.

Section 2: The Basics of Project Management

In this section you'll get a basic overview of project management. It includes important fundamentals for anyone beginning to learn about project management. If you're already experienced in project management, it's a good idea to review this section as a refresher.

Section 3: The Basics of Lean

Here you will get a basic overview of Lean methods. These important fundamentals will help anyone beginning to learn about Lean. If you're already experienced in using Lean, it's a good idea to review this section as a refresher.

At The Flying Machine, Inc., light bulbs come on for the project team members as they discover what caused their past projects to fail, and they learn how to set up new projects for success.

Section 4: Lean Project Management in Action

Refer to this section to see the combination of Lean and Project Management methods at work. The project team goes through all the steps in a project's lifecycle, and they apply Lean principles along the way. At the end of each phase in the project's lifecycle the team summarizes how they made that phase of the project Lean, and the benefits of doing so.

Section 5: Epilogue

In this section you will see how the story wraps up by illustrating the success of the project, what the team learned, and that the payback for practicing Lean Project Management is real.

Appendix A: Health Evaluation for Lean Projects

This checklist, called Health Evaluation for Lean Projects (HELP), is designed for leaders, sponsors, and project managers to use and ensure a Lean project is on track for successful completion. Use it to check a project's health during every phase of the project's lifecycle. When you can answer "yes" to the items on the checklist, you can feel confident that you're practicing Lean Project Management.

Finally, to assist you with getting started and with using standard work throughout every phase of your project, download free project management templates at www.PMtrailblazer.com.

Section 1

THE FLYING MACHINE, INC.

Terrible Tuesday

What started off as a normal Tuesday at The Flying Machine, Inc. had taken a downward spiral and become a terrible day. It all went south when Paul, the project manager for the hottest new product, presented a monthly status update to the leadership team. He was dreading this day, because he knew he had to present bad news that no one wanted to hear.

Over the past several months his project had been slipping further and further behind schedule. At the same time, the costs were increasing to beyond the allowable spending limit. Paul and his project team had brainstormed about how to get the schedule and cost back on track, but nearly all their time had been wasted on ideas that didn't work. Attempting to meet the deadline, they had worked overtime. They even skipped over some of the planned product testing. To save costs they switched to lower grade materials, but that ended up causing a series of quality issues. It was evident the project would greatly miss its committed completion date and its cost target. And, due to compromised product quality, their customers wouldn't receive the value they had been promised.

Because of the increased costs and the late completion date, the new product no longer met the profitability goals that had been set at the beginning of the project. And if the project was completed,

The Flying Machine would lose money instead of making the profits they originally expected.

After Paul shared the bad news, Emma, the CEO, looked at Eamon, the director of product development. "I don't know why we didn't see this coming. This is an incredible blow to our profitability this year, not to mention the relationship we have with our customers. We need to cut our losses." With a frown, Eamon nodded in agreement.

Before the end of that day, Paul and his project team got news from Emma that the project they had been dedicating all their time to, for over a year, was canceled. From then on, the team referred to that day as Terrible Tuesday.

Paul, greatly embarrassed and distraught from the pressure of the failed project, turned in his resignation the next morning. He thought he would be fired soon anyway, so resigning seemed like the only logical thing to do. Eamon and the remaining project team members felt a mix of guilt and frustration. They all wondered how long they would have their jobs.

The Flying Machine, an innovative high-tech company, designed and manufactured commercial unmanned aerial systems made up of unmanned aerial vehicles (otherwise known as drones), and the ground-based controllers that communicate with the drones.

Emma and Eamon had trusted Paul to deliver the newest drone on time and within the targeted cost. Now, Emma would have to explain to customers why they weren't going to get the new product they had been promised. Regardless of who the project manager was, this was not the first time a Flying Machine project was late, over budget, and did not meet their customers' expectations. Needless to say, Emma was not happy.

She met with the customers and was able to smooth things over with them – for now. After thinking about the failed project for a few days, Emma decided it was time to make a significant organizational change. "Should I replace Eamon?" she wondered. After all, bringing new products to completion on time, within their budgets, and meeting customer expectations was his department's responsibility, and the success rate wasn't good. Eamon was a technical specialist, one of the best vertical takeoff and landing engineers in the industry, but he was not as good at managing projects or meeting the customer's expectations.

After some thought, Emma decided to keep Eamon, but to talk things through with him and see if they could come up with a good plan for an organizational change.

The next morning, she stopped by Eamon's office. She didn't hold back in sharing her opinion with him. "We need to introduce new, high-tech products, but we can't afford to keep managing their development the way we have been. We have great business strategies as well as great marketing and sales plans. Our technology is more advanced than our competitors' technology. We have the best subject matter experts and manufacturing capabilities in the industry. But we're pretty lame at developing and delivering new products on time and within their cost targets. I'm not convinced we even know what we're doing wrong that ultimately gets us into these predicaments."

Feeling guilty, Eamon shrank a little in his chair and thought for a few seconds. "You're right," he replied. "If we knew what we were doing wrong, we would fix it. We need to replace Paul with a new project manager. We need to find a successful project manager, someone who can deliver most of the time."

Emma wasn't convinced this was a good enough solution. "I think we should find a person with a great level of experience who can help us understand what we're doing wrong and lead us in the right direction. I think we should hire someone at the director level to do this."

While Eamon was disappointed that getting a new director would mean losing a good portion of *his* responsibilities, he understood the need for the change. He was also relieved that he still had a job.

Emma continued. "We need a person with a strong project management background, since project management focuses on meeting schedule, cost and performance targets, and The Flying Machine has been failing in all these areas. But I wonder if there is any other expertise that could help us?" She paused, but Eamon didn't suggest anything. "I'll look into it, and let you know when we have some interviews scheduled," she promised.

As Emma stood up and opened the door to leave, she found Charles, the manager of manufacturing, raising his hand to knock on the door.

"Hello," he greeted her. "Have I missed anything?" He flashed her a smile to cover his curiosity.

"I'm thinking about how we can improve the development of new products," Emma said, looking him right in the eye. "If you have a suggestion, this is a good time to let me know."

Charles couldn't believe it. *Finally,* he could make his point! "Last year, we started applying Lean principles to manufacturing. While some people only see the yellow lines on the factory floor now" — he didn't even bother glancing at Eamon — "it's really helped us. The way we manufacture our products is easier and more cost effective. We're saving time, and there are less problems than we had before. It wouldn't hurt to spread those benefits around the rest of the company. I could help with that."

"I've read your reports, and I'm happy with the progress you've made," Emma responded. "And our manufacturing staff likes the new way of doing things, now that they're used to it." She smiled at Charles. "That Lean course you took has really paid off. Let me think about it."

Charles handed Eamon a couple of sheets of paper. He sometimes preferred to deliver reports in person instead of sending them by email; walking through the halls and talking to people let him hear more about what was going on in the rest of the company. "Here's that information you asked me for. The new engineering change will hold up production while the new parts are made by the supplier and shipped to us. See you later."

That afternoon, Emma started researching Lean Project Management online, and decided that the Flying Machine needed more than a project management expert. *What the company really needs, she thought, is a project manager who is also a sensei – a teacher of Lean principles who guides a team through the journey of applying Lean. That would cover all the problems we're having and teach us how to handle other projects in the future.*

Emma, Eamon and the Max, the Director of Human Resources, interviewed a dozen candidates, but each person was an expert in either project management or Lean methods, but not both.

And then, one day, they met Sam.

Sam arrived early for the interview. She was experienced, articulate and confident. She had a strong project management background and a strong Lean background, with credentials in both.

Emma didn't sugarcoat the current situation as she described the problems The Flying Machine was having. "We keep missing deadlines. We go over the project budgets. We haven't met our customers' quality or performance expectations. And even worse, we don't know what we're doing wrong that causes these things to happen."

Sam gave an empathetic nod.

Emma continued, "When we sell a product that is launched later than planned and costs have gone over the budget, we leave a significant amount of potential profits on the table. To make matters worse, our quality isn't great, so we lose money doing things like re-working defective products, mailing replacement parts, and trying to keep our customers from being mad at us. We need someone who can show us how to do things correctly."

Sam was busy taking notes. She looked up and asked, "Do you know if anyone has been documenting the lessons learned from past projects?"

Emma wasn't sure. "If we *did* document any lessons learned, I doubt we'd know where to find them."

"Do you have any *current* state value stream maps?"

Emma wasn't sure about that either. "If so, I've never seen them."

Sam looked up from her notepad. "Has anyone attended project management training or Lean training?"

Emma felt better about answering this one. "Yes! Our lead engineer has taken a class on project management, and our manager of manufacturing has taken a class on Lean. But that's pretty much it."

Sam thought for a moment and commented, "I feel confident that if I can meet with people and ask questions, I can help identify all the reasons why The Flying Machine projects miss deadlines, go over budget, and don't meet quality and performance goals. After that, I can work with everyone involved to come up with the right techniques to apply to future projects."

That was exactly what Emma wanted to hear. A few trusted people in her professional network had recommended Sam, and now she understood why. It didn't take long for Emma to decide that Sam was the right candidate. The next day, she offered Sam the job.

New Beginnings

Sam was excited about the opportunity to help The Flying Machine. She had solved many similar problems and led many projects before, but none that involved the development of drones. She had imagined creating drones since she was a child, and she was excited as she thought this could be her dream job.

Emma confirmed with Sam that her new title at the Flying Machine would be Director of Program Management. One of Sam's new responsibilities was to figure out what caused The Flying Machine's new product development teams to miss deadlines, go over budget, not meet performance goals, and not deliver the value that they had promised to their customers.

The other part of her job was to lead a team of project managers who were managing new drone projects. This would include teaching them project management skills they hadn't learned on the job, as well as how to apply Lean methods.

Managing new drone projects meant overseeing the execution of every step, from the concept phase all the way through factory production and into customers' warehouses. This included an exciting and all-new replacement for Paul's project. It was The Flying Machine's flagship project, with the internal code name

NBT, or Next Big Thing. NBT would be a new drone with an all-new, cutting-edge microprocessor.

Sam couldn't wait to get started. She knew that she could really make a difference within the company.

During the first week, she met individually with just about everyone involved with the company's new products. She asked questions, and more questions, and then even more questions. She sat quietly in meetings and listened, to learn how things were being done. She watched designers sketching out new product ideas, programmers designing new code, engineers drawing computer generated 3D models, and factory workers using all sorts of tools to put products together on the assembly lines. She complimented people on the good work they were doing, and she listened carefully as they described their challenges.

Sam also met with all the people who had worked on Paul's project. Although she had never met Paul, she felt bad for him, understanding the challenges he had faced and thinking that it wasn't all his fault that his project had failed. Each of the team members described that Terrible Tuesday and the struggles that led up to it. Her emphasis on listening, and not blaming anyone, encouraged everyone to be more trusting and to give her more information. The team members also discussed problems they had encountered with other past projects. Sam worked with the team to create a list of four common problem-causing themes, which they all began to refer to as "The Terrible Tuesday List."

At the end of the week, Sam met with Emma to discuss the list, and how each of the items contributed to the team's inability to meet deadlines, cost targets and quality expectations.

Emma responded, "Great work, so far. I completely agree with the list and would like to add one more item: customers are not getting what they expect." So, Sam completed the list of five common themes.

> ### Five Reasons that Caused The Flying Machine Projects to Fail
>
> 1. Time was wasted while trying to solve the wrong problems.
> 2. Projects were disorganized.
> 3. It took too long to get decisions made and approved.
> 4. Status updates were complicated and confusing.
> 5. Customers did not get what they expected.

"What I propose is that we move forward with the coming NBT project as our example of how to apply both Lean and project management methods to overcome these problems," Sam suggested. "While the team is learning Lean and project management skills, they'll develop a profitable product. It will be finished on time, within budget, within quality targets, and meet customer expectations."

Emma thought for a moment. She felt uneasy about using The Flying Machine's biggest and most important project as a sort of guinea pig to prove out the new approaches Sam was suggesting, but she knew that big changes were badly needed. The company needed the NBT project to succeed. She couldn't afford *not* to make big changes, and she trusted Sam to guide The Flying Machine through them. "Well, we have to start somewhere, don't we?"

Emma took the opportunity to explain the NBT project in more detail. "Krisha, a top-notch programmer we hired three years ago, has been developing and fine-tuning a cutting-edge microprocessor. After years of proving out this concept, it's ready to be added as a key feature in a new product. Our largest competitor, Tornado Inc., has been working on a similar technology for years, but with no success.

"Introducing a drone with this new technology would be a technical breakthrough for us and for the drone industry. It would generate significant sales and profits, not to mention that it would solidify our reputation with customers as a high quality, high-tech company. There are already customers interested in buying it." She paused for a moment.

"You have my support to use this project as an example of how to apply Lean Project Management, and to integrate it with project management methods. But, at the same time, please remember how critically important it is to deliver on time, within cost, and at the expected performance levels. Let me know when I can help."

Sam replied with a smile. "Thanks. I appreciate your support, and I will let you know when you can help." She thought, *this is a great way to wrap up the week. I want to get this project started right away.*

The NBT Team

Sam started preparing for the NBT project. With the exception of Sam, the people assigned to the project were the same people who had worked on Paul's canceled project. The team was multicultural, with people from North America and other places around the world.

Sam – Director of Program Management

Sam, experienced in Lean and Project Management, was the new Director of Program Management. She couldn't wait to solve The Flying Machine's existing project problems and then continue leading the development of new products on time, within their budgets, and delivering the expected performance levels.

Eamon – Director of New Product Development and the Project Sponsor

An innovative company like The Flying Machine needed expert leadership with creativity and a high-level understanding of technology. Eamon was the Director of New Product Development. He came from The Flying Machine's satellite location in Scotland for a two-year assignment. He was the keeper of the total budget for new product development and was the sponsor of the NBT project. Before Sam was hired, Eamon oversaw all project management. He had little formal training in project management, so he had been relying on the tribal knowledge passed on to him over the years. He was intimated by Emma's recent hiring of Sam, but he was relieved to have more time to focus on technical matters, which was his core strength and his main interest. He didn't want to worry any more about the details of project management.

Kyle –Lead Mechanical Engineer

Kyle provided engineering work on Paul's project. He lived in the same neighborhood as Paul and had gotten to know Paul. After witnessing Paul's struggles and resignation, Kyle wasn't sure how much longer he wanted to continue working at The Flying Machine. He thought the previous project's problems weren't Paul's fault, but were caused by a lack of direction and support from the management. He was glad to know that Sam supported using project management methodologies. But he didn't see any reason for practicing Lean, which wasn't surprising since he didn't really know anything about Lean. According to Kyle, the only noticeable outcome of using Lean at The Flying Machine was the yellow lines painted on the factory floors. Regardless, he was willing to give Sam a chance.

Krisha – Lead Electrical Engineer and Programmer

Krisha developed and fine-tuned the cutting-edge microprocessor that The Flying Machine needed to stay ahead of its competitors. She divided her time between the U.S. headquarters and her family home in Bangalore, India. She was a quiet person of few words, but when she spoke up, people listened to her. She asked thought-provoking questions and offered better than average ideas.

Charles – Manager of Manufacturing

Large and loud, Charles had a reputation for being arrogant and stubborn. He frequently irritated people on the team. On the previous project they nicknamed him *"Stink Bomb,"* because he would often stop by a meeting that was already in progress, and drop some alarming project related news without suggesting any solutions. Then he would abruptly leave because he "had to be somewhere else," leaving the team to investigate the issue without him.

He took a lot of flak from other employees at the Flying Machine who were convinced his only useful Lean contribution was to paint yellow lines on the factory floor.

Charles was an advocate for Lean but didn't understand or trust the use of project management. It seemed like too much work for what it was worth. He expected that Sam would want him to follow some project management mumbo jumbo that would waste boatloads of everyone's time, especially *his* time.

He was protective of the factory and was on a personal mission to keep the project team from under-designing a drone that would require last-minute modifications and upset the flow of other products being assembled in the factory.

Adam – IT Specialist

Adam was recruited from a local university about two years earlier. He learned quickly and was already a technical whiz at everything from spreadsheets to websites. He'd always been willing to help solve problems, which his coworkers appreciated.

Jean-Francois – Director of Marketing and Sales

Jean-Francois worked closely with customers to determine their needs and wants. He gathered their pricing expectations, desired features, and expected delivery dates, and shared that information with the team. Although he lived near the company's headquarters, he often traveled back to see his extended family in the south of France.

Sam met with Eamon and briefed him on her plan to use the NBT project as an example of how to apply Lean Project Management methods. She needed to assign someone as the project manager, a person who would lead the team and also be completely open to Sam coaching and mentoring the team through the entire duration of the project. Unfortunately, none of the existing project managers had much experience, and some of them had seemed less than excited to learn about Lean techniques when Sam had chatted with them. Sam and Eamon agreed that this would be a great opportunity for Kyle to learn how to be both a good project manager and good *Lean* project manager. It would also give him more options for developing his career at The Flying Machine.

The next day, Sam met with Kyle. She described everything she knew about the coming NBT project. She explained, "I'd like you to serve as the project manager. I'll be a coach and mentor on the project, showing you and the team how to practice Lean Project Management. This will broaden your expertise, and it could also benefit your career by opening other doors, if you want it to."

Kyle was excited about the opportunity to lead such a large, important project, but he was also concerned. He had a small amount of project management experience, but would it be enough? He was concerned about what had happened to Paul, and Kyle was also skeptical that practicing Lean would be helpful. He asked, "Is the goal to have a Lean project or a Lean product?"

"Both," Sam replied. "Lean skills, coupled with project management methods, will enable us to meet our committed delivery date, our cost target, and our performance objectives. At the same time, we'll remove waste in our processes, saving us and our customers excess costs. Once our customers receive their new products, we'll all feel comfortable that they received the best possible value." She paused. "And we'll be evaluating everything along the way, just like you evaluate the engineering of new jobs you've been given. So if anything starts causing problems, we'll be able to catch it *and deal with it* before it blows up into a huge problem."

Kyle thought to himself, *this is a giant culture change for The Flying Machine. I wish we'd been able to fix the problems the last time we worked on developing a drone.* He was anxious, but he trusted Sam to lead the changes necessary to successfully complete the project. He was eager to learn and willing to take on the challenge. He accepted the project manager role. During their first coaching session, Sam and Kyle decided to begin their journey with a review of the Terrible Tuesday list.

The Terrible Tuesday List

1. Time was wasted while trying to solve the wrong problems.
2. Projects were disorganized.
3. It took too long to get decisions made and approved.
4. Status updates were complicated and confusing.
5. Customers did not get what they expected.

"We'll address each item on the Terrible Tuesday List with Lean Project Management solutions," Sam reassured him. She explained that the NBT project's goals and deliverables had not yet been confirmed, and that they would need to be finalized in the coming weeks. "You'll need assistance from the team members with finalizing the goals and deliverables, creating a high-level cost estimate, and developing a preliminary project schedule." Kyle thought it sounded like a reasonable way to get started.

PROMOTING LEAN PROJECT MANAGEMENT

The next Monday, Sam pulled the entire team together. "Welcome to the NBT project! I'm looking forward to working with everyone." She described what she knew about the project and then continued. "This project will be different from past projects in that we'll be practicing Lean Project Management. To accomplish that, we'll start by taking some time to learn about both project management and Lean."

The team members looked at each other with curiosity.

"Kyle will lead the team as the project manager, and I will serve as a coach and mentor as we learn about and apply Lean and project management skills."

Kyle nodded in agreement. Then he told the team that the project's goals and deliverables had not yet been confirmed but they would be finalized in the coming weeks. "I'll need your assistance with finalizing the goals and deliverables, creating a high-level cost estimate, and developing a preliminary project schedule."

The team members nodded in agreement, except for Charles. He looked annoyed. "We don't have time for all of this. We have a boatload of work to get done!"

Sam responded, "You have a good point, Charles. However, every person on our team plays a critical role toward reaching success. Each person needs to have a full understanding of how to contribute their part, or it will take us much longer than necessary to get our work done."

Jean-Francois gave them another point of view. "To be honest, our customers want their suppliers, like us, to practice Lean. If I can tell them we're practicing Lean, they'll have a greater respect for us, and they'll think we know what we're doing." The team members chuckled. "They already assume we're practicing good project management, so we should make sure we truly are."

The team seemed open to the idea of learning about both, and they wanted to know when the learning would start.

"Before we start formally working on the project, we'll complete project management learning sessions followed by Lean learning sessions. And we'll start tomorrow." They were surprised by Sam's sense of urgency but nodded in agreement.

The next day, the team members met for their first project management learning session. Once everyone was seated, Sam began.

Section 2

THE BASICS OF PROJECT MANAGEMENT

What is Project Management?

"Welcome, everyone, to 'The Basics of Project Management.' Let's start by describing what project management is. Can anyone help me out with this?"

Adam raised his hand. "I think it's when a project schedule is created that shows all the project steps from the beginning to the end."

Sam smiled. "Thank you, Adam. Creating a detailed schedule is included in a project management plan, and there's much more."

"You're practicing project management when you plan and execute your projects to meet their intended cost, schedule, and quality objectives. Project managers in the business world also make sure their project's deliverables are accepted by the customer, be it an internal customer, external customer, or both, and that there are minimal or no disruptions to other work within the organization."

Adam shook his head. "I've never managed a project. It sounds tough."

Krisha spoke up. "Neither have I."

Sam raised her eyebrows. "I bet you have. Practically everyone's a project manager. Even if you're not a *career* project manager, chances are, you've probably managed some type of project in your personal life, making you a project manager at some level." She gave some examples of everyday people who, probably unbeknownst to them, are also project managers.

A vacation planner

"If you're planning a vacation, you are a project manager. You have a goal to get away and have some fun, and you have a plan to meet that goal by selecting your destination, finding a rental car, a hotel, getting airline tickets, coordinating activities, determining who will take care of your home while you're gone (getting mail, watering plants, feeding the cat, etc.). You will need to manage your vacation costs and ensure that everyone on the trip has their expectations met. Doing all that is project management!"

A car buyer

"If you're buying a car, you are a project manager. You have a goal, even if it's only in the back of your mind, such as what specific kind of car you want. You also have a plan on how to meet that goal, such as finding the car within a certain timeframe. You plan to test drive some cars and how to pay for a car, even if it takes several years of payments. You even plan to ensure that the car has a minimum quality threshold — you want certain features, and you need a car that's going to get you from A to B without breaking down. Doing all that is project management!"

A college student

If you're a college student, you're a project manager. You have a goal — graduating with a specific major — and within a certain timeframe. You have a plan to meet that goal, to attend classes, and pass exams. This also requires a certain level of quality, including a minimum grade point average, and all within a certain cost – including potential student loans."

"As you can see, there are many ways in which someone could be managing projects. The list could go on and on and include things like managing the creation of an art project, renovating a room in your home, building a shed, or running for public office. If the work you're doing has a goal, requires coordination, has a cost and an end date, it's a project."

The team members seemed relieved to know they had some experience in managing projects after all. Sam walked toward the markerboard. "Let's keep going."

THE TRIPLE CONSTRAINT

"Project managers are always prioritizing items known as limits or constraints, such as cost, schedule and scope, along with other important factors like project risks, resources, quality and customer satisfaction.

"When tracking the progress of a project or providing status updates, the minimum information project managers typically provide is an update on the project's cost, schedule and scope. Cost, schedule and scope make up what's known as the triple constraint."

Sam drew a picture of a triangle on the markerboard.

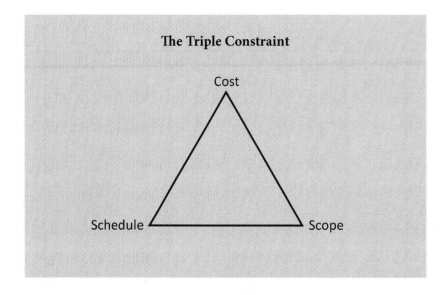

As she finished drawing the triangle, she turned to the group. "This is one of the most important concepts to remember about project management. In geometry class, we learned that if one leg of an equilateral triangle changes in length, one or both of the other legs of the triangle will also change. Similarly, when one of the items in the triple constraint changes, one or more of the other items will change too.

"For example, if someone requests an additional product feature (additional scope) that wasn't in the original plan, the project cost will likely increase in order to pay for that feature and to have additional resources work on developing that feature. The delivery schedule will likely be delayed because it will take extra time to develop and test that new feature.

"Project managers who embrace this concept will be better at estimating the impact of requested changes, better at negotiating what changes can be made, better at managing risks, and better at accurately communicating the true status of their projects. When changes are requested, it's important for the project manager to see how the time, cost, or scope would be impacted, and then communicate the impact to stakeholders.

"Project managers and team members who don't grasp the impact that changes have on time, cost, and scope are likely to uncover serious issues when it's too late to fix them!"

The team members nodded in agreement because they had just experienced that on their previous project.

"Let's cover one more topic today."

The Five Phases of The Project Lifecycle

With a straight face, Sam asked the team, "Have you ever worked on a project that seems like it's drifting and has no end?" The entire group laughed.

Krisha sat up. "That happens all the time here."

Sam smiled at her sympathetically. "I've experienced that too. All projects should have a formal beginning and a clear end date that all team members and stakeholders are aware of. To help understand where to start and where to end a project, let's look at the overall lifecycle of a project."

"Throughout the life of a project, there are five important phases: Initiating, Planning, Executing, Monitoring and Controlling, and Closing." She returned to the markerboard and drew another diagram.

The Project Lifecycle

Initiating	Planning	Executing	Closing
Monitoring and Controlling			

"The first phase is the Initiating Phase. These are the typical activities that should take place during the Initiating Phase." She began writing as she read aloud each of the activities.

INITIATING PHASE

- Confirm there is an initial Business Case
- Assign a project manager
- Gather historical project information
- Understand the cultural environment, existing systems and policies
- Define the project goals, and create a project charter
- Conduct a formal project Kickoff Meeting

Adam looked curious. "Are we in the Initiating phase right now with the NBT project?"

"Yes!" Sam was happy he was still paying attention. "Once we complete the first five items in the Initiating Phase, we'll conduct our project Kickoff Meeting."

While the team members knew they would have lots of future questions, they were engaged with what Sam was explaining, and they were content to have her continue. Charles was impressed that the project management methodology, at least so far, meant spending time up-front to make sure the project was well organized, and that further work didn't start until a good foundation was set.

"Next comes the Planning Phase." Sam began writing and read aloud each of the included activities.

PLANNING PHASE

- Finalize the project charter and have it formally approved by the project sponsor
- Select team members
- Determine, agree to and document everyone's roles and responsibilities
- Develop a project management plan

Adam noticed the second point. "But us team members are already here in this room!"

Sam explained, "We have the *primary* team members here. Once we've spent more time identifying all the work to be completed, we'll identify any additional subject matter experts (SME's) or other team members we may need. We'll also document each team member's specific roles and responsibilities."

"The next phase is called the Executing Phase." Sam began writing as she read aloud each of the included activities.

EXECUTING PHASE

- Perform work according to the plan
- Manage stakeholders' expectations
- Team building and conflict resolution
- Manage contracts, select suppliers
- Track and address issues
- Execute risk mitigations and contingency plans
- Implement process improvements
- Track and report progress to the sponsor and stakeholders

"This phase looks easy compared to the first two phases," Kyle commented.

Sam shrugged. "Well, it should go according to plan if we build a strong foundation. That means completing everything in the Initiating and Planning Phases first."

Charles sat up and spoke loudly. "You mean no nasty surprises? No firefighting?" He had been unusually quiet up to this point. "Firefighting is what we do every day here, it seems. It's the norm. Unfortunately, we're good at it."

Sam replied. "Good planning upfront – even if we need to spend extra time doing it — should result in few or no nasty surprises or firefighting." Charles pulled a pen out of his shirt pocket, clicked it, and started to take notes. He had never experienced this type of project planning, and he liked what he was hearing.

"The next phase is the Monitoring and Controlling Phase, *but* the activities listed here shouldn't wait for the first three phases. These activities should take place throughout the project and especially during the Execution Phase." Sam began writing and reading aloud each of the activities it included.

MONITORING AND CONTROLLING PHASE

- Measure performance and compare it to the initial base-line – take corrective actions as necessary
- Meet intermediate milestones
- Track and report progress and performance
- Control scope – manage approved scope changes
- Monitor new and revised processes for effectiveness
- Monitor stakeholder engagement

Jean-Francois raised his pen in the air. "I've seen the word 'stakeholder' a few times today. What exactly is a stakeholder?"

"A stakeholder is anyone who's impacted by our project. They may be positively or negatively affected. In either case, they are a stakeholder."

Krisha chimed in. "So, it's more than just our team?"

"That's right. It's the people in the factories, our customers, end users, and more. I'll talk more about that soon. We'll also identify them all in a Stakeholder Assessment.

"The fifth and final phase is the Closing Phase." Sam began writing and reading aloud.

CLOSING PHASE

- Confirm all work is completed according to the charter document
- Receive feedback and acceptance of all project deliverables by the sponsor and customer
- Hand over the final product for sustainability, maintenance, and continuous improvement
- Close contracts and purchase orders
- Release resources to work on other projects
- Document the final lessons learned
- Present a final progress report

Charles sat up. He couldn't stop himself from shouting. "Hold on here! Are you saying we're going to take time to think about continuous improvement?" This was music to his ears. "I thought only Lean experts gave a hoot about CI. And are you saying we're going to document the lessons we've learned?"

Sam grinned, enjoying his surprise. "Yes, and yes. In fact, we won't wait until the end of the project to document the lessons we've learned. We'll take time in-between and at the end of our major milestones to document what went well and what we recommend doing differently next time."

Charles was so impressed he was speechless. He couldn't believe his ears and eyes. He thought to himself, *I like where this is going. Daayuum! If we actually do these things, I'm personally going to become a project management advocate.*

Sam was happy with everyone's interest in learning. "Those are the five phases within the lifecycle of a project that teams go through as they manage their work. We've covered quite a bit today. Are there any more questions?"

SYNCHRONIZING WITH THE PRODUCT DEVELOPMENT PROCESS

Eamon's voice emerged from the back of the room. "Brilliant! This is quite helpful." He came to the meeting after it started and had been quietly sitting in the back, sipping tea, and taking notes. "But are you suggesting we replace our Product Development Process with the five phases in the lifecycle of a project?" He was concerned because The Flying Machine's leadership team had spent a long time perfecting their Product Development Process.

Sam replied. "No! But I can see why you would ask. Let me show you how they work together." Sam took a few minutes to describe how the processes would work together.

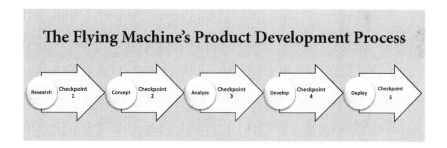

The Life Cycle of a Project

Initiating	Planning	Executing	Closing
Monitoring and Controlling			

"The project management phases happen in parallel with our product development process," Sam explained.

"The Product Development Process is a *governance process,* meaning that checkpoints are in place at every step to make sure all the product development steps are followed. A formal approval is required at each checkpoint before the team can proceed to the next step. It's a necessary roadmap to guide us in the development of a product, but it does not include the steps necessary to manage a project."

"Each phase in the lifecycle of a project is also a formal process. While there can be some overlapping of project lifecycle phases, the important work in each phase needs to be completed before fully moving on to the next phase."

Eamon looked relieved to hear that the project lifecycle would happen parallel to the existing product development process. "Brilliant. That makes sense."

"Great. Are there any other questions for today?" Sam looked at everyone. "We can certainly revisit any of these topics at any time. Tomorrow we'll meet at the same time, same place, and we'll cover what's included in a Project Management Plan. See you then."

The Project Management Plan

The next day, Sam greeted the team. "Welcome back! Today we'll cover what's included in a Project Management Plan.

"Sometimes people mistakenly refer to a *project schedule as a project management plan.* A project management plan includes much more information than just the schedule. According to the Project Management Institute, an international governing body on project management, project managers should leverage ten important areas of specialization, or knowledge areas, when they create a project management plan." She wrote on the markerboard and read aloud each knowledge area:

1. Stakeholder Management
2. Resource Management
3. Cost Management
4. Schedule Management
5. Scope Management
6. Risk Management
7. Communication Management
8. Quality Management
9. Procurement Management
10. Integration Management.

Adam looked concerned. "This is an INSANE amount of responsibility and work to do!"

Sam smiled. "It *is* a large amount of responsibility. Project managers are responsible for all these areas *and* for being a good leader of the team. But they're not an expert on every subject, so they need to rely on their team members, who *are* subject matter experts, to offer their input. The project manager needs to be working on these tasks full-time, and the team members need to offer their expert advice when it's needed."

Adam looked relieved.

"Let's take a deeper look at each of the areas within a project management plan, starting with Stakeholder Management."

STAKEHOLDER MANAGEMENT

"Stakeholders are people or organizations who are involved in or impacted — either positively or negatively — by a project. When we practice Stakeholder Management, we identify all the stakeholders and keep them satisfied, engaged, and informed throughout the life of a project. There are some helpful tools we'll use to identify and manage our stakeholders. We'll cover those a little later."

Krisha was concerned. "What happens in the scenarios where we identify all our stakeholders, but then they leave and get replaced by new stakeholders? On our last project, the quality director agreed with everything we were doing throughout the project. Then he left the company and we got a new quality director. As we were finishing the project, we found out the new director wasn't satisfied with what we were delivering. We spent months having to re-do a ton of work we thought we had already finished."

"Responding to changing stakeholders is definitely a challenge," Sam agreed. "We'll need to work together to make sure we manage all our stakeholders' expectations — even the stakeholders who change during the project. This doesn't necessarily mean we make any and all changes they request. It means we need to have excellent communication with them throughout the project. We'll need to listen to their input and let them know what to expect so they're not surprised later."

There weren't any questions, so Sam continued. "Next, let's look at resource management."

RESOURCE MANAGEMENT

"The term *resources* can mean human resources, also known as people, or it can mean other physical means of getting project work completed, like tools, or machinery, or equipment. It's the project manager's job to take the lead and work with you to determine which resources are needed throughout the life of a project.

"It's important for each person on the team to understand their role and what their responsibilities are throughout the life of the project. Each team member should also know when they need to start working on the project and when they're expected to roll off the project. If needed, the project manager will negotiate with the manager of the resources needed to get the right quantity, skillsets, and timing of available resources.

"We'll need each of you to help form a cohesive team, communicate with each other, and quickly resolve any potential conflicts within the team."

Kyle was a little relieved that Sam described this as *the project manager's responsibility AND the team members' responsibility.* Each of the team members, including Charles, took note of how THEY had a key responsibility to make a cohesive team. It wasn't just the project manager's job.

COST MANAGEMENT

"Cost management involves estimating the initial cost of a project and then managing any cost variances that occur throughout the project's life. It's the project manager's responsibility to meet committed cost targets by controlling costs along the way and reporting any variances. The project manager needs input and ongoing support from all team members.

"Often, during the Initiating Phase of a project, there many *unknowns,* making it difficult and even uncomfortable to provide a cost estimate. Cost assumptions are made, and the project manager provides the best possible estimate.

"But once the project manager and team learn more about the project, the estimate can be fine-tuned to include more realistic details. The project manager will need to make decisions, such as whether certain work can be completed internally or whether it's necessary to outsource that work. Other project costs may need to be considered and fine-tuned as well, like travel expenses, consulting fees, equipment, overtime pay, software licenses, and more."

Everyone was taking notes, so Sam paused for a minute to let them finish. When they were ready, she continued. "Next up is schedule management." She watched as several people perked up and seemed even more interested.

SCHEDULE MANAGEMENT

"Schedule management involves estimating the amount of time it will take to complete a project and then managing any schedule variances that occur during the life of the project."

Charles looked skeptical. "But what if someone else already gave an estimate of how long it will take? I've been burned plenty of times because I couldn't meet someone else's schedule commitment that was way too optimistic."

"I understand why that would be a problem, and I bet we've all experienced it at some point." Sam saw the team members nodding and looking even more interested. "If another person has pre-determined a project's duration, it's the project manager's responsibility, with the team's input, to confirm that the schedule is realistic — or revise it if necessary — before moving into the project's Execution Phase. Once they commit to meeting that date, the project team needs to develop a plan to make it happen."

Charles seemed content with that answer. "That's fair. As long as the team can weigh in."

Sam continued. "A good schedule contains intermediate milestones. Meeting or beating intermediate milestones gives everyone confidence that the overall project deadline can be met.

"Who has created a work breakdown structure?" There was silence. "Have you *ever heard* of a work breakdown structure?" No one had.

"I'll explain that. A work breakdown structure, known as a WBS, is a visual depiction of the all the project work, broken down into manageable pieces or *deliverables*. It looks somewhat like an organization chart, but it contains the project deliverables instead of people's names or roles. It's created by the project manager with the team's input.

"Once the WBS has been created, the team works together to estimate the how long it will take to design, prototype, test, revise, test and finalize each of the deliverables, and the logical sequence in which to complete them. This information is critical for creating an effective schedule.

"The WBS will spark team discussions on what each of the deliverables will cost, which people should work on what, the risk level of each deliverable, how to best communicate the status of each deliverable, and more. This will all come together soon when we go through it together as a team."

"No more running around in circles?" Adam asked. "That could save a lot of time."

"We're actually going to know what we need to do before we start trying to do it. That's like the way we organize our work before we start coding a computer program," Krisha commented.

"Yes! That's right. And you can imagine how much time it saves when people know what they need to do, and when, and who is working on it with them." Sam was pleased that the team was getting involved, and actively discussing the process. "Let's move on to something that you're all familiar with — handling changes after the work has started."

SCOPE MANAGEMENT

"Project scope is the work necessary to complete a project. Think of project scope as having a fence around your project. Deliverables inside the fence are included as part of your project, but items, features, and requests outside of the fence are not part of your project. Items within the fence are *in scope,* and items outside of the fence are *out of scope.*

"We're practicing scope management when we define all the work and the requirements necessary to complete our project, and then we make sure all of it (and only the in-scope work) is completed. It's important for the project scope to be clearly defined and approved *before* the work begins, otherwise we'll risk spending time and money working on the wrong things.

"Sometimes, even when the project scope is clearly defined up front, features later get added, removed, or redefined, and team members start doing unplanned work. This is called uncontrolled (outside of the fence) scope and is also referred to as scope creep."

Jean-Francois spoke up. "But shouldn't we *dazzle our customers* by giving them a few extras?"

Sam looked concerned. "Not if it's not part of the original, agreed-to plan, because once the charter is agreed to, we'll be committed to a cost target and a scheduled completion date. Adding extra features, often referred to as 'gold plating,' that the customer didn't ask for, could put our project at risk for overspending and not delivering on time, not to mention that the extras may not even dazzle our customers. Once a customer sees that we over delivered, they may think they are over-paying and demand a price reduction."

Charles jumped in. "We only want to deliver what our customers are *pulling*, or in other words, expecting."

Jean-Francois thought about that for a few seconds. "I guess our customers would be pretty happy if, for once, we just delivered what we promised, when we promised it, and for the price we promised. Sadly, it doesn't happen often."

"Scope management means that no changes to the project's scope are allowed without first going through a formal change control approval process." Sam began writing. "Here are some questions we'll need to address."

SCOPE MANAGEMENT DECISIONS TO MAKE

- For this project, what is in scope and what is not in scope?
- Is there an existing change control process we can use, or should a new process be created?
- Who should investigate the impact of requested changes to determine whether, and how, they might impact our project's cost, schedule, scope, quality, safety, or customer satisfaction?
- Who should decide if the requested changes should be approved?

"To avoid potential disasters, the team will need to think through, and make sure there are answers to, each of these questions. We'll do this during the Planning Phase, before starting the execution of our project."

Charles thought to himself, *this is a great amount of thinking and a massive amount of work. But I guess it makes sense. Geez, if we don't do this, our project will be a hot mess, just like the ones before it!*

"Along with controlling the scope of the project, we also need to manage risks," Sam told them. "Let's talk about risk management."

RISK MANAGEMENT

"Who has participated in a Risk Assessment?" she asked. No one spoke up.

"What is a risk?" Krisha spoke up. "Is it when something bad could happen?"

"Thanks for asking that, Krisha. Yes. A risk is an event that may or may not occur, but if it does, it could impact our project. Most likely, the impacts would include unpleasant surprises like schedule delays, cost overruns, quality concerns, unhappy stakeholders or customers, and more.

"The project manager, with the team's support and input, needs to proactively address risks before they become a reality. This may seem like a difficult task, but there are some helpful tools to use. We'll use them when we get to the Planning Phase of the project."

Jean-Francois looked curious. "But what if something already occurred? Is it still called a risk?"

"That's a great question, Jean-Francois. The term risk is sometimes confused with the term *issue*. A risk is uncertain. It may or may not occur, whereas an issue did occur. If, by chance, there are any issues identified during our coming risk assessment, we'll document them separately so they can be addressed. And we'll develop an action plan and assign an owner to take on the issues."

They seem confused when I talk about risk, Sam thought. Once we start planning the project, I'll need to take some extra time to illustrate why managing risk is so important.

COMMUNICATION MANAGEMENT

"Communication management involves the collection, creation, storage, monitoring, and distribution of project information. To best communicate with our stakeholders, we'll need a Communication Plan.

"Who has participated in the creation of a Communication Plan?" Sam asked. She wasn't surprised when no one spoke up.

"A common rule of thumb is that project managers spend about 90% of their time communicating, if not more, throughout the life of a project. It's the project manager's job, with your input, to create an effective communication plan. The plan is a document of who to communicate to, what to communicate, when and how often to communicate, and what methods to use for communicating." Kyle looked a little concerned, as if he hadn't expected that this would be part of his job. Sam turned back to the markerboard and read aloud as she began writing.

Communication Plan

Who – which stakeholders?
What – what is the message?
When – when should this be communicated?
How (medium) – what's the best way to communicate it?
How Often – what's the frequency for communicating it?

"When we get to the Planning Phase, we'll create a communication plan together, as a team." Kyle was writing furiously, making sure he got it all down.

"Let's take a quick break, say five minutes, and then we'll get into quality management." Sam smiled, then headed across the room to get some coffee.

QUALITY MANAGEMENT

Charles was waiting for this part. He was sitting on the edge of his seat.

"Welcome back," Sam said. "*Quality* is defined as the degree to which a project fulfills its requirements. We should deliver according to the quality we committed to." She paused while Jean-Francois wrote that down.

"It's important to understand the difference between building quality into our project versus inspecting our project later to see if it meets our expectations. Building quality in is called quality assurance, and inspecting for defects later is called quality control. Both are important, but if you don't practice quality assurance, it may be too late to make corrections for defects found later."

Charles stood up and raised his arms. "Amen and hallelujah!" He was so loud he startled the others in the room. Even people in the conference room down the hall could hear him. "I get SO tired of people expecting the factory to inspect and fix things that that should have been built in!" He paused for a moment and asked, "Is this truly part of project management? Because if it is, you have my support one thousand percent!" He couldn't believe it. "Daayuum! Who knew that was part of project management?" The team chuckled at his excitement.

Sam smiled. "Yes, it is Charles! We'll document the expected quality, and then we'll practice quality assurance by building that quality in. If we do a good job, there will be few, *if any,* defects found during the quality control inspections later. We'll take some time to determine what kind of quality assurance metrics to use throughout the project to assess whether our deliverables are meeting our customer's quality expectations."

Charles shared his experience. "During our more successful previous projects, we checked the quality of our product designs during intermediate milestones — the earlier the better, I think. We used simulation software first, then product prototypes, and then pre-production samples that resembled the final product. If we only relied on final inspections during manufacturing, we wouldn't be able to recover the potential lost time due to a failed quality test. We tested in our lab, and we also asked a select group of future consumers to test the products under actual use conditions. Of course, we needed to make sure the prototypes and pre-production samples used for testing were a close simulation to the final product, and we also needed to ensure the test samples were safe for our customers to use."

"Thanks, Charles. Those are great examples." Sam was happy that Charles was so engaged.

She continued, "We'll need to focus on quality and prevent any unpleasant surprises. Unpleasant surprises, especially when they're found later in a project, often result in unmet schedules, costs overruns, and unhappy stakeholders. Other issues could arise as well, like damage to a customer relationship, or a product safety recall, which could tarnish our company's image, or worse." The team looked alarmed, except for Charles.

Charles felt compelled to convince the team. "The paradox is that when you spend more time defining and building quality into your project, you save the time you would have spent problem-solving and reworking items."

Kyle spoke up. "But what if someone changes their mind later in the project and expects a different level of quality?"

Sam answered with the empathy of experience. "Sometimes, midway through a project or even later, stakeholders *do have* differing opinions of what quality means on a project. Since quality is defined as *the degree to which a project fulfills its requirements,* it's critical that those requirements be documented clearly and up-front in the project charter and/or scope statement. If a change is requested, the project manager should work with the team to estimate what the impact would be on the project cost, schedule and scope. In other words, we should refer to the triple constraint. The requested change should go through the change control process.

"We'll need to determine the right metrics to use so we, and all the stakeholders, know how quality will be measured along the way. If we do a good job of defining, documenting, and measuring quality along the way, there should be little or no debate about what quality means, thus reducing the odds of encountering unpleasant surprises."

The team looked relieved.

"Now, let's move on to Procurement Management."

PROCUREMENT MANAGEMENT

"Who knows what Procurement Management is?" Sam asked.

Krisha responded, "Is it when you need to buy stuff for your project?"

"Yes, that's a part of it. Procurement management involves the creation of relationships with outside suppliers of goods or services that are needed for a project. Making a purchase for a service usually starts with a documented and detailed description of the work to be completed, called a *statement of work,* or SOW. The SOW is a formal contract that's usually created by a subject matter expert, but it's reviewed and ultimately agreed to by the project manager and possibly others.

"Purchase orders are also formal contracts. If the team needs to purchase items, it's important to read and understand the 'fine print' in the purchase orders, since they typically include agreements on price (cost), delivery (time) and deliverables (scope)."

Krisha responded louder than usual. "The triple constraint!"

"That's right, Krisha. Without fully understanding and agreeing to procurement contracts, including purchase orders, it would be impossible to effectively manage our project's cost, schedule or scope." Sam again drew a picture of the triple constraint.

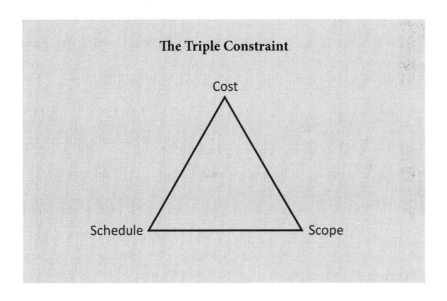

"Let's wrap up today's session with one final topic."

INTEGRATION MANAGEMENT

"The pieces of the project plan don't happen one at a time. Many activities happen at the same time, like a juggler tossing and catching several balls in the air. So it's important to know how to balance and prioritize all this work. The tenth knowledge area, Integration Management, is necessary when some or all of the knowledge areas are happening simultaneously and need to work together.

"Once we get started on our project, many things will be happening at the same time. Decisions in some areas will impact other areas. It's going to get seriously busy. But if we all work together, as a cohesive team, we can be in control every step of the way while balancing and prioritizing the work as necessary." The team looked a little frightened, but everyone nodded in agreement.

Adam sat up. "It sounds like you could sum up the project manager's job by saying they manage integration."

Sam smiled. "You could say that."

She thanked everyone for their engagement during the session. "Tomorrow will be our third and last day for the Project Management Learning Session. See you then."

On the third day, Sam welcomed everyone back. "Today I'd like to go over some common project management terms, but before that, I'd like to take a few minutes to discuss some of the different types of organizational structures."

Organizational Structures

Sam turned to the markerboard and read aloud while she wrote.

Organizational Structures

Functional
Projectized
Matrix

"Some organizations have *functional structures,* meaning that projects and project teams are managed by the functional leaders of specialized departments. Another organization type is called *projectized.* This is the structure used when a company is mostly organized around its projects and all team members report directly to the project manager. A third and common type of organization is called a *matrix organization.* In a matrix organization, project team members report to two leaders; their functional department leader and the project manager of the projects they've been assigned to."

Krisha was curious. "It seems like our organizational structure is the matrix type."

"Yes, that's right Krisha." Sam responded. "While people report to their functional managers for their specialized work, they report to the project manager for projects they're assigned to.

"It's important for project managers to know what type of organizational structure they're working in, so they understand their authority level. It also helps a team understand who their stakeholders are. For example, the functional managers are stakeholders. We'll need to keep them informed about our project. It's the project manager's job to give them status updates and to continue getting their approval to have you work on the project.

"The functional managers will probably ask Kyle to weigh-in on your performance evaluations."

When Adam heard that, he stopped playing on his phone and sat up in his chair.

"Let's learn some additional terms everyone on the team will need to know."

Additional Project Management Terms Everyone Should Know

"We've already covered some of these terms, so I'm sure you could already describe those. I'll run through each one and you can let me know if you have any questions." Sam turned to the marker-board and as she wrote, she named each term aloud.

Project
Program
Portfolio
Project Manager
Stakeholder
Sponsor
Project Charter
Scope Creep
Lessons Learned
Work Breakdown Structure
Risk
Issue
Gantt Chart
Critical Path
Kickoff Meeting

PROJECT

"A project is simply any planned undertaking that is meant to achieve a goal. Projects have a definite beginning and an ending, and each project is unique in some way compared to other projects."

PROGRAM

"A program is a group of related projects. The projects are typically grouped together for a business reason."

Adam was intrigued. "Is that really all it is? I always thought there was something more complicated around what a program actually is."

Sam clarified it for him. "Some organizations give different names to different kinds of projects and roles, perhaps calling a large project a *program* or calling a project manager a *program manager.* But the actual definition of a program is a group of related projects. There's no need to make it any more complicated than that."

"That was easy," Adam mumbled. He liked to mimic the voice from the old Staples® commercials. The rest of the team chuckled.

PORTFOLIO

"A portfolio is a group of related programs that are typically grouped together for a business reason."

"Seriously?" Adam was again intrigued.

"You got it," Sam assured him.

Kyle pointed to Adam as if to cue him. "That was easy," Adam grinned.

PROJECT MANAGER

"A project manager leads a team in the planning and executing of a project."

Krisha jumped in. "That description sounds like it's a super simple job, but we know it's the project manager's job to juggle the *whole* project management plan throughout all *five phases* of a project's lifecycle, and that is no simple job!"

Sam smiled. She was proud of Krisha for remembering what she learned.

STAKEHOLDER

"A stakeholder is a person or an organization who is impacted by a project, either positively or negatively."

SPONSOR

"A sponsor is usually a leader in an organization and one who selects a project manager to lead a project. The sponsor provides funding for the project, agrees to the deliverables documented in the charter, agrees (early in the project) on the final acceptance criteria, and ultimately signs off on the completed deliverables."

All the team members looked at Eamon. "I guess since I provide the funding, I'm the project sponsor for the NBT project." He was learning how important his role was.

Sam agreed, "Yes. That's right. And there are many more sponsor responsibilities." She knew that inadequate sponsor support was a common cause of project failure, so she wanted to make the next points clear for Eamon.

"Here are the sponsor's responsibilities listed by each project phase." She spoke as she wrote on the markerboard.

Sponsor Responsibilities

Initiating Phase
- Select the project manager
- Establish the vision for the project and ensure it's aligned with the Business Case goals
- Set a project completion timeframe
- Provide funding and confirm the project cost target (budget)
- Review and formally approve the Project Charter, including approving the final the acceptance criteria

Planning Phase
- Communicate project priorities
- Secure resource availability
- Review the Risk Response plan
- Ensure there is efficient decision-making

Executing, Monitoring and Controlling Phases
- Evaluate project status alignment with the Business Case goals: continue the project commitments or cancel the project?
- Protect the scope of the project
- Actively engage with the project manager
- Provide visible support for the project
- Communicate project status to the sponsor's peers
- Communicate potential changes in the business that could impact the project
- Serve as an escalation path to resolve conflicts if needed

Closing Phase
- Review the final status report and ensure that the Business Case goals were achieved
- Accept the final project deliverables
- Ensure the customer benefits and value are realized
- Provide input into the lessons learned

Eamon and the team members were shocked. They had no idea the sponsor had so many responsibilities. Meanwhile, Kyle was relieved that someone else besides him was accountable for the project's success. He thought to himself, *if we had followed this plan on our past projects, the previous project manager Paul would still be here.*

Eamon wanted clarification. "So I need to agree upfront to the charter, which at that time should include the acceptance criteria?"

Charles looked at Eamon and added his opinion. "That makes sense. If you don't agree on the plan up front, how would any of us know we're working on the right things? How would we know when we're finished with the project?"

Eamon nodded in agreement. The importance of his role was still sinking in.

"That's right," Sam confirmed.

During past projects, the team *generally* knew what they were supposed to work on, but there were no formal charter documents to confirm that. It was common for projects to stray off course since there had been little documentation to help guide the team toward fulfilling their original commitments.

Sam continued, "The sponsor also serves as a point of escalation. If there is an issue the project manager and team cannot resolve, the project manager should escalate it to the sponsor — as soon as possible, while there's still time to address it."

Charles looked at Eamon again. "The project sponsor has a boat-load of project accountability."

Eamon, still surprised, agreed. "I get it. I'm here for the team."

PROJECT CHARTER

"A project charter is a formal document that describes the goals of a project, what the project will deliver, when it will be delivered, the allowable cost, and who the key stakeholders are. It may also include some assumptions about the project and any known risks. It is usually created by the project manager with input from the team's subject matter experts. The project charter is created during the Initiating Phase of a project and should be formally approved by the project sponsor before the project planning begins."

Charles spoke up. "What if the charter needs to be revised after the project is underway?"

Sam explained, "The charter should be specific enough to describe the project, but general enough that it doesn't need to be revised or re-written — unless there is an approved major change to the scope and deliverables. In that case, the project manager or sponsor should either revise the charter or create a new one. Of course, any changes to an existing charter should be formally approved by the sponsor and then communicated to all of the stakeholders."

SCOPE CREEP

"Scope creep happens when uncontrolled or unmanaged changes occur within a project after the project charter has been approved. Everyone on the team, including the sponsor, needs to take responsibility for controlling the project's scope. If a change is requested, it should go through the scope change control process."

The team members looked at each other as if they could read each other's minds. *Do we have a scope change control process?*

LESSONS LEARNED

"Lessons learned are insights gained from a project that are gathered and documented, so they can be used as a reference for future projects. We shouldn't wait until the project is over to document the lessons learned. They should be documented at least after each project phase. We'll document what went well and what we would recommend doing differently next time. It's not about placing blame, but about helping the next project team so they work more efficiently."

Charles saw this as an opportunity to trace this topic back to Lean methods. "It sounds like when we document lessons learned, we enable the next project team to be Lean."

Sam smiled. "You're absolutely correct."

WORK BREAKDOWN STRUCTURE (WBS)

"We learned what a work breakdown structure is when we learned about creating project schedules. Creating a WBS is the preparation work needed for creating a project schedule, a cost estimate, a risk assessment and a resource plan.

"It's created by the team as a visual breakdown of the project into smaller components." She showed everyone an example of a WBS template.

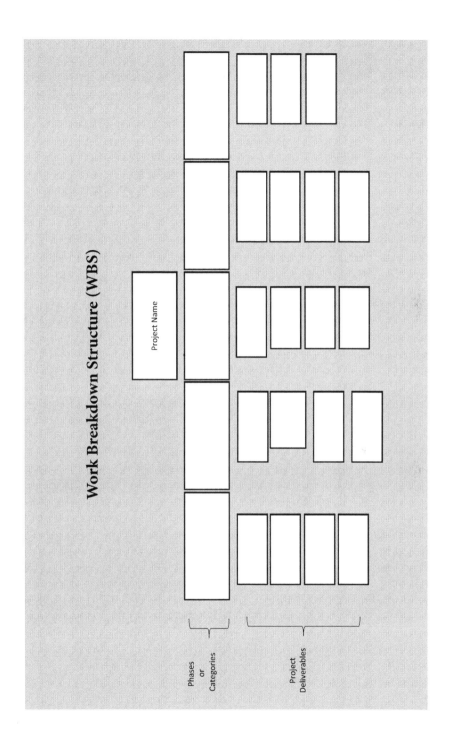

"When it's completed, the team can see all the major work of the project at a glance." Everyone nodded in agreement.

RISK

"A risk is an uncertain event which has a probability of occurring. If it does occur, it could impact the project. *Risk management* is the process of identifying and assessing project risks and then creating proactive plans to minimize the impact to the project if the risk occurs. If risks are not identified and mitigated early in a project, they can become issues later. A risk that has already occurred is no longer a risk, but an issue."

ISSUE

"An issue is a situation with negative consequences. It could also have been a previously documented risk that turned into a reality. It may be recoverable if it is quickly and properly addressed. We'll need to document issues as they occur by keeping an Issue Log to record all project issues and the status of their resolutions."

GANTT CHART

"A Gantt Chart is a type of horizontal bar chart used to show a project schedule, where each activity in the schedule is represented by its own horizontal bar. The width of each bar indicates the duration of that activity. A Gantt chart can be a helpful visual aid to quickly understand a project schedule." Sam shared an example of a high-level Gantt chart showing the lifecycle phases of a project.

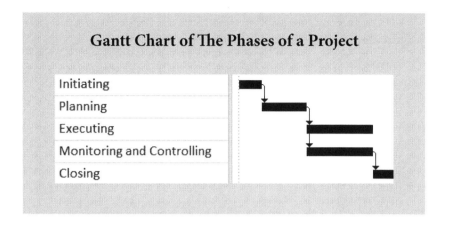

Gantt Chart of The Phases of a Project

Initiating

Planning

Executing

Monitoring and Controlling

Closing

CRITICAL PATH

"Sometimes we're asked how fast our project can be completed." Sam smiled as Eamon nodded his head in agreement.

She continued, "Before we can answer that, we need to know the critical path – the list of tasks that will take the longest to finish, or have the longest task durations, in our project. This is important because reducing the amount of time it will take to achieve non-critical path items, the shorter tasks, will not shorten the overall duration of our project. We need to focus on saving time on the most time-consuming tasks during the project.

"Once we've identified the critical path, if we want to shorten the overall project duration, we'll need to be creative and think of ways to shorten the tasks that are on the critical path.

"We'll need to be careful. We may be asked to reduce our project's schedule and even receive 'help' by stakeholders naming some features or work that could be removed from our project in order to speed up its completion. This is great if the items to be removed are on the critical path, but if they aren't on the critical path, our project can't be shortened if they are removed.

"Each of us needs to understand the items on the critical path to know whether the total duration of the project can be shortened or not. We need to be able to explain this to the people requesting changes as well."

Jean-Francois chuckled. "I always thought items on the critical path were the features the customer wanted the most."

"No, the critical path is the path with the longest task durations." Sam clarified.

KICKOFF MEETING

"When starting a new project, the Kickoff meeting is the first formal meeting held by the project manager. Typical attendees include the project team, key stakeholders, the project sponsor and possibly the customer. During this meeting, the project manager reviews the project charter, making sure everyone has a common understanding of the project deliverables. It's a great time to answer questions, set project ground rules, and introduce team members and stakeholders who may not have worked together before."

Since she had presented all the terminology, Sam wrapped up the meeting. "And that concludes our project management learning sessions. I hope you found them to be helpful. There will be much more to learn once we begin to put these concepts into action. Are there any other questions?"

Kyle raised his pen in the air. "When should we have our Kickoff meeting for the NBT project?"

"After we complete the items in the Initiating Phase – especially the project charter. You'll review the charter in the Kickoff meeting."

Kyle nodded as if he agreed.

Sam continued. "Thanks, everyone. On Monday we'll begin our next subject: The Basics of Lean."

Section 3

THE BASICS
OF LEAN

What is Lean?

The following Monday, the team shuffled back into the conference room. This time it was to hear what Sam had to share about Lean. "Welcome back, everyone. Over the next few sessions, we're going to learn a lot about Lean techniques, and from now on we'll just call it Lean. Let's get started."

Sam explained. "Lean is a philosophy, or way of thinking and acting."

Charles occasionally liked to tease Kyle. "Kyle, Lean is not about doing the least amount of work compared to everyone else."

Sam ignored the comment and continued. "When people in an organization think and practice *Lean,* they focus on providing value that their customers are willing to pay for. They strive to eliminate waste wherever possible. They're always on the lookout for ways to maximize productivity, and they focus on continuous improvement. They also show respect for people."

Charles felt a twinge of guilt for teasing Kyle. *I guess I wasn't showing respect,* he thought to himself.

Sam continued, "In an organization with a Lean culture, this is work that everyone is responsible for.

"The term *Lean* started back the 1980s."

This part worried Sam a little, because some of the team members hadn't even been born then. She wasn't sure if they would be interested.

"It was a way of describing the methodology that helped Toyota run at maximum efficiency following a severe energy crisis in the 1970s. Toyota managed to survive and thrive after the energy crisis by creating a culture of empowerment and continuous improvement.

"But why apply Lean to project management? Because applying Lean principles to projects results in lower project costs and faster completion times, with an increase in project quality and customer value. We'll talk more about applying Lean to project management a little later."

Krisha couldn't wait to ask a question she'd been wondering about. "Is Lean the same thing as Six Sigma?"

Sam was excited that Krisha was interested. "That's a good question Krisha, and a common question. The answer is that they can overlap but they're not the same."

The Difference between Lean and Six Sigma

"Lean and Six Sigma are complementary," Sam explained. "Lean is about eliminating waste, for example, eliminating unnecessary steps in a process, while focusing on customer-defined value.

"*Six Sigma* is a tool used to identify and control variations in processes. When it's used successfully, Six Sigma eliminates the defects — waste — caused by variations and thus increases value for the customer. The goal of Six Sigma is to ensure there are no more than 3.4 defective parts per million (PPM) in products or processes delivered. A defect is defined as anything that is not acceptable to the end customer."

Kyle remembered how Sam described quality assurance as quality that is designed in, not inspected in. It would be up to his team to design in great quality for the NBT project. Then he thought about The Flying Machine's biggest competitor, Tornado. They were known for having quality issues. We can do better. *We'll design and build quality in, and then control variability.*

Sam went a little deeper. "The reason it's called Six Sigma is because it aims to be six standard deviations, or amounts of variation, between the mean (the average) and the nearest specification limit in any process. The symbol for standard deviation is the Greek symbol Sigma. Six standard deviations equal Six Sigma, or 3.4 defective PPM."

Krisha asked, "Why Six Sigma and not five or seven or more sigma?"

Charles rolled his eyes because he thought Krisha's questions were getting annoying. But at the same time, he was curious to hear the answers.

Sam replied, "It's more about aiming for perfection and eliminating defects than it is about reaching a certain number. Six Sigma is a near-perfection goal that is very difficult to achieve, let alone exceed. Some companies invest in and strive to reach Six Sigma. Other companies aim for a more achievable goal – as it may not be worth it for them to spend the time, cost and effort to achieve a quality level that may not provide a return on their investment." Krisha nodded with acceptance.

Sam continued, "Organizations may practice *Six Sigma,* combine *Lean with Six Sigma* and call it Lean Six Sigma, or they may use other terms like *Operational Excellence,* or *Zero Defects* for the same goal, which is to aim for near-perfection."

Kyle remembered a previous initiative at The Flying Machine called "Operational Excellence." He hadn't been part of it and didn't fully understand it. But now he was catching on to what it meant. *Now I see what they were trying to accomplish,* he thought to himself.

Sam told them, "The *Six Sigma problem-solving methodology* is often used within the Lean framework and includes five basic steps." She turned to the markerboard and wrote:

D M A I C

Define
Measure
Analyze
Improve
Control

"We'll cover each of these in more detail later."

"Six Sigma practitioners have different roles within a Six Sigma project, defined by their belt levels. She turned to the marker-board and wrote:

Six Sigma Belt Levels

Yellow Belt
Green Belt
Black Belt
Master Black Belt

"According to the American Society for Quality (or ASQ), the following organizational roles correspond to types of certifications. To become certified, a person must meet certain requirements in order to take the certification exams. Each certification requires having a minimum amount of experience to take the exam, a minimum exam score, and more." She shared the following chart with the team.

Six Sigma Certifications

Type of Certification	Role in Organization
Yellow Belt	Participates as a project team member and subject matter expert, and reviews process improvements that support the project.
Green Belt	Assists with data collection, analysis, and problem-solving, and leads small Six Sigma projects or teams.
Black Belt	Leads problem-solving projects, trains, and coaches project teams by following the DMAIC model.
Master Black Belt	Trains and coaches Black, Green and Yellow Belt practitioners. Develops key metrics and strategic direction. Acts as an internal consultant.

"Many organizations offer training and certifications in Lean or Six Sigma, or Lean Six Sigma. Not all certifications result in colored belts. For example, some Lean organizations offer Bronze, Silver and Gold certifications. Some offer certificates after passing an exam, and some offer certificates just for attending training classes.

"Any additional questions?"

Kyle was impressed by how organized and prepared Sam was. He didn't understand how to apply everything he learned yet, but he agreed that much of what Sam had described so far would be good to practice alongside project management.

Sam continued, "Let's review the Eight Forms of Waste."

The Eight Forms of Waste

"What is waste?" Sam asked the team.

Krisha was the first to respond. "To spend unnecessary time or money?"

"Yes, you could say that. From a Lean perspective, *waste* is non-value-added activity. It's any step taken — but not absolutely required — to complete a process, product or service. When waste is removed, only the value- added steps that are required for the customer will remain in the process. There are eight forms of waste."

Kyle looked overwhelmed. "Eight different things to remember"?

Sam smiled. "Let me share a helpful tip. One way to remember the eight forms of waste is by using the acronym DOWNTIME." Everyone started writing DOWNTIME. "Here's a table that shows each form of waste and examples of project related waste."

Eight Forms of Waste

Acronym	Form of Waste	Example of Project Related Waste
D	Defects	Mistakes that require rework. A poor design or poor documentation that did not meet expectations the first time.
O	Overproduction	Producing more than is needed or producing something before it is needed. Overdoing or overthinking tasks, spending more time than required.
W	Waiting	Waiting for project work to begin, waiting for approvals, supplies, etc. Not having a clear approval process, requiring too many approvals, waiting for communications.
N	Non-Utilized Talent	Poor assignment and communication of roles and responsibilities, underleveraging subject matter experts, lack of teamwork.

Acronym	Form of Waste	Example of Project Related Waste
T	Transportation	Wasted effort transporting items, not co- locating team members, far away work areas.
I	Inventory	Having excess materials, work in process, or finished goods. Having information sitting in files or in databases that are not being utilized or worked on. Having too many people for some tasks.
M	Motion	Any wasted motion to move parts or people. Traveling to meet with team members, searching for or sorting information. Recreating work due to lack of stan-dardization. Not storing team documents in a com-mon location, resulting in extra searching.
E	Excess Processing	Doing more work than is necessary. Addressing prob-lems without under-standing the root causes. Gold plat-ing – providing features the customer does not require. Excessive reports.

PROJECT MANAGEMENT WASTE

Sam had hit a nerve, which took the team members down memory lane to that Terrible Tuesday when their previous project was canceled. Many of the examples listed in the "waste" column in the chart had happened during that project.

She kept going. "We need to be careful because it's easy for waste to occur in projects. Here are a few examples." She listed them on the markerboard:

- Projects that have unrealistic schedules or costs
- Projects that include unclear or unnecessary requirements
- Inefficient meetings
- Lack of knowledge transfers between people
- Not knowing where project bottlenecks are
- Interruptions to workflow
- A non-existent or ineffective scope change control process

Everyone looked discouraged, as they remembered each one of these problems happening on past projects. But Sam reassured the team, saying "I'll show you how to eliminate project-related waste in the coming learning sessions."

Kyle was hooked. He couldn't wait to learn more.

The Five Whys

The next day, Sam welcomed the team again. "Today we'll start with the Five Whys." Kyle had his pen out and was ready to take notes.

"The Five Whys approach is a simple method for solving problems. Why do *we* care? Because sometimes people waste significant amounts of time trying to solve a problem when they haven't taken the time to understand the root cause of the problem.

"Use the Five Whys to find the root cause of a problem by asking a sequence of 'Why?' questions five times.

"Why *five* times? Well, five is actually just an arbitrary number. The point isn't the number, it's the probing. Once the first 'Why?' is asked, the answer forms the basis of the next question. To get to the root of the problem you may need to ask two times or maybe ten times. The point is that you shouldn't take the first answer as the solution. Keep asking 'Why?' until you're satisfied you've found the root cause. Since not all problems have a single root cause, it may be necessary to uncover multiple root causes." Then Sam drew a diagram for them.

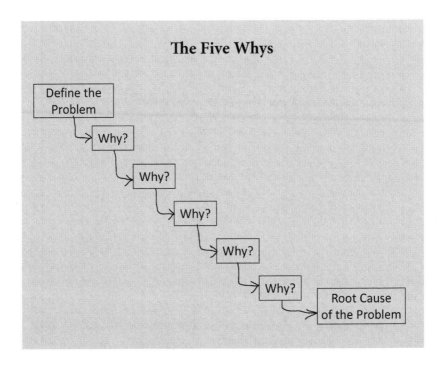

The Five Whys

"Let's go through an example of finding the root cause of a problem by asking at least five whys. I'll make up a pretend problem." She looked at Kyle. "Kyle, our customer just canceled their order." She leaned over and (loudly) whispered to him. "This is where you ask the first of at least five whys."

Kyle responded. "Oh, okay. Um, why?"

"Because we had a pattern of not delivering our product to them on time."

Kyle responded. "Why? Why were we not delivering on time?"

"Because we spent several weeks re-working products that didn't pass quality control inspections."

"Why? Why didn't they pass the inspections?"

"Our supplier shipped us defective component parts."

"Why? Why did they ship us defective component parts?"

"Because there's a global shortage of the specific raw material we specified, so our supplier used an unauthorized substitute material."

"Why? Why did they use an unauthorized material?

"Because we didn't provide our supplier with a list of pre-approved materials to use as a substitute in the event of a shortage. ROOT CAUSE!"

Kyle laughed. "I sounded like a three-year-old asking *why* so many times." The team laughed too. "But I can see how that approach could help get to the root cause."

Kyle thought about the first item on the Terrible Tuesday list. He remembered times when the team was busy addressing big problems, only to find out later that they hadn't identified the root cause of the problems before applying solutions. Because they didn't know what caused the problems, they wasted time coming up with the wrong solutions. He thought to himself, *this is such a simple approach. We should have tried this back then.*

He asked Sam, "As we move forward with the learning sessions, would it be alright if I post our Terrible Tuesday list, along with proposed solutions?

She nodded. "That's a great idea, Kyle."

On a flip chart, Kyle wrote "Terrible Tuesday Problems", with the first problem from the list. Then he wrote a proposed solution.

Terrible Tuesday Problems

1. Problem: time is wasted while trying to solve the wrong problems.

    Solution: use the Five Whys to confirm and find the root cause of a problem by asking a sequence of "why" questions, at least five times.

Sam continued. "OK, now you know about the Five Whys and how you can use that approach to confirm and get to the root cause of a problem. Let's talk about 5S."

5S

"5S is a methodology used to help build an organized and uncluttered work environment. It's called 5S because it includes five
steps, and each step begins with an 'S'. Anyone can apply 5S,
regardless of the type of environment they are in or the type of
work being done." She shared a chart with the team. "Applying
these five exercises results in a workplace that is well organized
for productivity."

5S

Exercise	Description
Sort	Eliminate anything that isn't needed by separating the needed supplies, tools, etc. from unneeded items.
Set in Order	Organize everything that remains by arranging and identifying items for ease of use.
Shine	Clean the entire work area.
Systematize	Schedule regular maintenance.
Standardize	Form new habits that become standard.

Charles read through them all. "Looks like there's plenty of work for you, Jean-Francois!" he said. "If you practice some of these, you might unbury your desk one day." Jean-Francois gave Charles the side-eye.

Sam continued, "Keep in mind that this isn't only about our physical work areas. Are your electronic files stored in a neat and tidy place where you and the rest of the team can find the most current version of them — in a matter of seconds?"

Kyle's eyes got bigger has he thought about how terribly unorganized his electronic files were. "I'll admit it. There's a whole lot of 5S needed in my life too."

Adam saw this as an opportunity. "I think I could help with organizing the team's electronic files, and then set up a shared database with team member access."

Sam responded, "That's great, Adam."

Kyle jumped in also. "I'll take you up on that when we get started with the project."

Kyle thought about some of his previous projects. Work staging areas and testing areas had been so disorganized that he constantly spent time looking for important files, papers, and tools. Sometimes the team purchased new tools because they couldn't find their existing tools in all the clutter. They even re-created documents because they couldn't find versions they had already created.

He spoke up. "It would be extremely valuable to apply 5S in commonly used areas, like storage rooms, supply rooms, and labs."

Charles chimed in. "Has anyone been in the battery test lab lately? It's a shitstorm!"

Krisha couldn't stay silent. "Oh my gosh! I don't know what happened in there, but I can't even go in there anymore. I'm not mentioning any names, but some people are paying to outsource their battery testing just so they can avoid going into that disaster of a room!"

Sam raised her eyebrows. "OK then. I guess we know where to start with our first 5S exercise, don't we?"

Everyone chuckled.

Kyle walked to the flip chart and wrote the second item from the Terrible Tuesday list.

2. Problem: projects are disorganized.

   Solution: apply 5S to create a workplace that is well organized for productivity. Sort, Set in Order, Shine, Systematize, Standardize.

Additional Lean Terms Everyone Should Know

Sam continued with, as she called it, "terms everyone should know." She passed around a reference list of terms to each person on the team and began explaining them.

Value
Value Stream
Value Stream Mapping
Continuous Improvement
Huddle
Muda, Mura, Muri
Gemba Walk
Flow
Pull
A3
Kaizen
Kaikaku
Yokoten
Nemawashi
Poka-yoke
Visual Management
Visual Management Boards
Visual Controls

Obeya
Just in Time (JIT)
Standard Work
Plan-Do-Check-Act (PDCA)
Define, Measure, Analyze, Improve and Control (DMAIC)
Voice of the Customer (VOC)

VALUE, VALUE STREAM AND VALUE STREAM MAPPING

Value

"Let's start with value. What do we mean when we say something adds value?" No one made eye contact with Sam.

"Value could be described as a good or service which meets the customer's needs at a specific price at a specific time. The customer defines value.

"As a team, and as a company, we always need to be focused on that value and what the customer is willing to pay for. Throughout the project, we should double check to make sure that what we're delivering has value from the customer's perspective."

Value Stream

"A value stream includes all the value-added steps, as well as any non-value-added steps necessary to take a product or service from its conception all the way to completion."

Value Stream Mapping

"A value stream map is a graphical representation of the value steam. To visualize a value stream, we need to create a map that reflects the current state of a process being used today. A value stream map flows from left to right, over time, with the process steps lining up in their order of occurrence. The value-added time it takes to complete each process step is noted below the map, as well as the non-value-added steps. To create the map, it's important to get input from experienced subject matter experts who know how the current process works and each of the steps involved from beginning to end.

"The map should always be made from the customer's perspective, and it should focus on delivering the customer's expectations." She shared a simple template of a value stream map with the team.

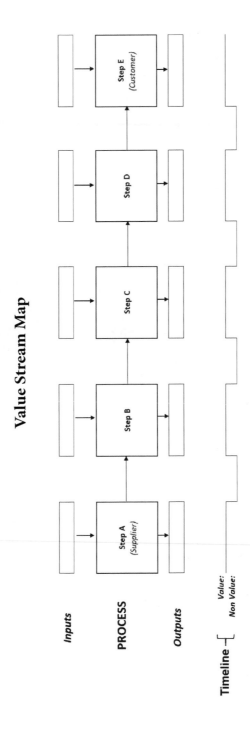

Value Stream Map

Sam explained, "For an activity to be considered as adding value, it needs to meet three criteria:

- The customer must be willing to pay for it.
- It must transform the project/product/service toward completion.
- It must be done correctly the first time.

"Anything else on the map would be considered non-value-added work."

Charles sat up. "We already know every process we follow in our company is messed up. We don't have value stream maps that reflect the current state of how things are done. Maybe we should lock ourselves in a room for a month and map them all."

Sam patiently replied, "It's good to select one *current* state process to map at a time. It's not good to map an entire operation or multiple operations at one time because in most cases, it's just too complicated."

Charles looked relieved.

Sam continued, "As a map is being created, issues within the current state process are highlighted. These are areas where a future *kaizen* event may be necessary. We'll get to that in a minute. After a map of the current state is created, it's used to find areas of waste as well as where value exists. Once it's clear where the waste exists, ideas are brainstormed about how to make process changes to eliminate the waste.

"Next, value is examined to see if it can be further improved. Then a *future* state map is created, representing how the process, ideally, should operate going forward. A good future state process map is a roadmap for improvement plans.

"To achieve success, the recommended changes need to be implemented. These could include things like eliminating wasteful steps, adding expertise, upgrading technology, changing policies and procedures, and more."

Kyle was already sketching out what the current state value stream process looked like for the NBT project. He couldn't wait to get the team involved.

CONTINUOUS IMPROVEMENT (CI)

"Improving our processes should be an endless pursuit. We need to constantly question the value of all our activities while we strive to eliminate waste. Our goal is perfection."

When Sam mentioned the word perfection, just about everyone in the room looked up at her like she was half crazy. She didn't flinch and just continued on.

HUDDLE

"A huddle, commonly referred to as a daily stand-up, is a short meeting that's usually held at the start of each day. It's used to check in with all the team members and discuss specific plans and goals for the day. It's important to keep to a set agenda so the meeting is short and efficient.

"The most effective huddles allow each team member the opportunity to share what they are working on and what challenges they may be facing. This approach promotes transparency, accountability, and the opportunity for team members to help each other accomplish tasks, if needed."

Kyle loved the idea of a fifteen-minute huddle every day to keep the team energized and focused on the highest priority items.

MUDA MURA, MURI

"The Toyota production system and the concept of Lean were developed to eliminate the three types of deviations that show inefficient allocation of resources." Sam wrote them on the markerboard.

> muda = wastefulness
> mura = unevenness, irregularity
> muri = overburden, excessiveness

"As we manage the flow of work that our projects consist of, we'll need to be aware of these three concepts. Our goal is the opposite of these – it's to have *fast flowing value*."

Kyle thought about how team members sometimes waste time when they don't know what to do (muda.) Some areas of work may not have enough resources (mura), and others may have too many resources (muri.) He liked the idea of identifying those problems and fixing them so the project could stay on schedule.

GEMBA WALK

"The purpose of a Gemba walk is to go to an actual place where work is happening. It involves respectfully observing any processes taking place, and the people doing their work, to gather data and facts for problem-solving and to improve processes.

"Gemba walks provide valuable insight into the flow of value through a company. They often uncover opportunities for improvement and new ways to support the people who are doing the work. The approach is collaborative. Employees provide details about how their work is performed, why they do what they do, and when they do it."

This was the first time that most of the team had heard of Gemba walks.

FLOW

"The concept of flow is simple. Once our future state maps are created, our goal is to generate continuous flow by eliminating opportunities for waste to re-enter the process. We need continuous flow with manufacturing processes, and we also need continuous flow with the way we manage our projects."

With a smug look on his face, Charles looked over at Kyle and pointed to his notepad to indicate he should write that one down in his notes.

PULL

"We want to avoid delivering value the customer has not requested. In other words, don't deliver more scope than the customer agreed to. We will let the customer be the one to pull the flow."

A3

"An A3 is a problem-solving method that is documented on a one-sided piece of international A3 (11" by 17" in the U.S.) sized paper. The idea is to fit the entire background of a problem – including a list of the root causes, proposed countermeasures, and other supporting graphic aids — all on one sheet of paper.

"An A3 page layout has room to list the problems and their root causes on the left side of the paper, and a list of countermeasures and next steps on the right side of the paper." Sam showed the team an example.

A3

Title: Date:

Background

Provide a brief background of the problem.

Current Conditions

Provide visual descriptions and describe/explain the problem.

Analysis

Identify the root cause of the problem. Use the Five Whys if needed.

Proposed Countermeasures

List countermeasures, options or actions. Specify in order of preference which countermeasures are recommended.

Next Steps

List recommended next steps to take next.

KAIZEN

"*Kaizen* is a Japanese term for *incremental improvement.* A kaizen event is a short duration team activity, that typically lasts no longer than a week. It starts with a specific process improvement goal that is intended to address specific problem areas identified in the value stream mapping process."

Sam looked at each person. "All stakeholders who are familiar with the area in which a kaizen event is taking place should be involved — from factory workers to project team members to executives.

"When we complete a current state value stream map, we use starbursts to highlight problem areas — or, in other words, where kaizen events are needed." She shared a sample value stream map with kaizen starbursts on it.

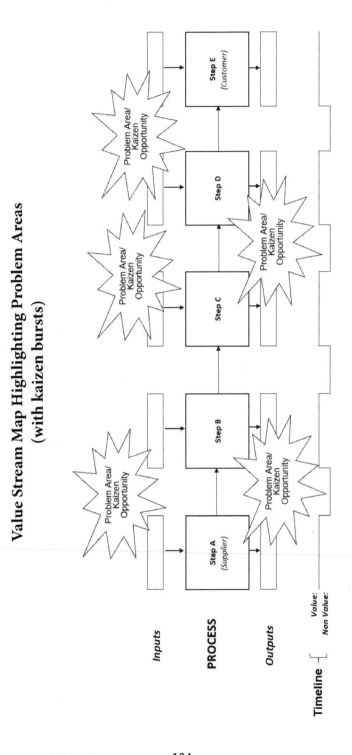

Value Stream Map Highlighting Problem Areas (with kaizen bursts)

Kyle couldn't resist. He walked to the Terrible Tuesday list on the flip chart to revisit the first item by adding more solutions.

1. Problem: time is wasted while trying to solve the wrong problems.

    Solutions:

    *   Use the Five Whys to confirm and find the root cause of a problem by asking a sequence of "why" questions, at least five times.
    *   Complete Gemba walks to fully understand how the work is being done. Closely observe the people and the processes and learn from them where the true problems exist.
    *   Use the A3 approach to document the root cause of problems and their suggested countermeasures.
    *   Complete value stream mapping of the current state to find areas of waste, where problems exist, and where kaizen events/improvements should be made.

Sam was happy to see Kyle's enthusiasm for applying Lean methods.

KAIKAKU

"Unlike kaizen, which is focused on incremental improvements, *kaikaku* is a Japanese term for radical change," she continued.

Jean-Francois jumped in. "But who wants an incremental change when we can have radical change? Wouldn't it be more effective to skip kaizen events and just focus on kaikaku events?"

Sam answered, "It is tempting, Jean-Francois. But a kaikaku event is more likely to be effective if some kaizen events have already been completed successfully."

YOKOTEN

"Yokoten is *a process of sharing rapid learning*. For example, if we hold a kaizen event and the results are successful, we should share those results quickly across our organization so they could be used in other areas. Our goal is to copy what works and apply it in other areas."

NEMAWASHI

"Nemawashi is a Japanese term for *the informal process of gaining consensus*. It involves carefully describing a proposed change, or a decision that's needed, by talking to stakeholders and gathering their support. This is something to do BEFORE going into a formal meeting. That way your formal meetings become *summary* meetings instead of *hope everyone agrees decision-making* meetings. The opposite approach would be to go into a meeting hoping everyone will hear your proposal for the first time and like it."

This sent a chill down Kyle's spine. He thought, *Ugh! I should have been practicing this. By NOT doing this, I previously set myself up for embarrassment, frustration and delays as key stakeholders didn't agree on topics during my meetings and wouldn't make decisions. Nemawashi, where have you been?*

He walked up to the Terrible Tuesday list again and added to the third item.

3. Problem: it takes too long to get decisions made and approved.

    Solution: Practice nemawashi. Talk to stakeholders individually. Describe proposed changes or decisions needed in order to gather their support, consensus, and decisions *before* inviting them to a formal meeting. Turn the formal meeting into a *summary meeting* versus a *decision-making* meeting.

POKA-YOKE

Sam was enjoying the team's interest in learning about Lean. "Our next term is poka-yoke. Poka-yoke means mistake-proofing or taking all measures possible to prevent mistakes from happening.

"Have you ever purchased an item that you had to build?"

Everyone nodded.

"Did you ever build it incorrectly?"

The whole team laughed. They all said "Yes!"

Jean-Francois told a story about the gas barbeque he bought last spring and then spent four hours putting together. When he was finished, the top was on backwards. The whole team looked at Jean-Francois with sympathy because they all remembered having a similar experience.

Sam told them, "The best designers and engineers practice poka-yoke. They design products that cannot physically be manufactured or assembled incorrectly. But poka-yoke isn't limited to product design. Hospitals and many other organizations add it to their processes to reduce or eliminate mistakes from happening. We can add it to our future state processes and procedures."

As you might have guessed, the terms visual management, visual management boards, and visual controls are all related to each other." Sam said. "Let's start with visual management."

VISUAL MANAGEMENT

"Visual management is a simple tool that quickly shows the current status to anyone, within, say a minute or less."

Kyle's jaw dropped. "Oh. My. Gosh," he said out loud. "Imagine if we could provide status updates that people could read in a minute." He thought about the long, boring meetings he often had to sit though. He smiled and raised his eyebrows. "That would be freakin' awesome!"

Sam smiled. "We can make that happen. We can even create project management documents like the project charter, risk assessment, communication plan, etcetera – each one readable, and understandable, within a minute. The next topics will help us to achieve that."

Kyle and Krisha looked at each other, wondering what would be coming next.

VISUAL MANAGEMENT BOARDS

"Visual management boards are important Lean communication tools that are used to provide information at a glance. There are several different types of visual management boards, including boards for project status, continuous improvement, and more. A board should always include up-to-date, relevant information, so it's best to use markerboards, chalkboards, or other mediums that can be quickly updated."

"Related to this is the idea of visual controls."

VISUAL CONTROLS

"Using visual controls involves using signs, graphics, or other forms of eye-catching displays instead of written instructions. They're typically displayed in places where information is communicated to large groups of people. The goal of using visual controls is to provide quick recognition of the information being communicated, in order to standardize, improve efficiency, and provide clarity."

OBEYA

"Obeya is a Japanese term for 'large room' or 'war room,' and it refers to a form of project management used in Asian companies. Throughout a project's lifecycle, the stakeholders get together in a large room to observe visual charts, graphs and more, to speed up communications and decision-making. The type of information displayed depends on the project, but it would include information like project milestones, status updates, and information to help facilitate decision-making."

Kyle was counting how many Japanese terms he had learned so far.

He smiled as he visualized all the most current project-related information that could be on display in an obeya room reserved specifically for the NBT project. He envisioned leaders and other stakeholders showing a sincere interest in what was being displayed. Up to this point, the only time stakeholders had seen project related information was during brief status update meetings.

He walked up to the Terrible Tuesday list again to address the fourth item.

4. Problem: status updates are complicated and confusing.

   Solutions:

   a) Use visual management, visual management boards, and visual controls (signs, graphics, or other forms of

> eye-catching displays) to help share and report information in a format that is easy to read and understand.
> b) Display the visual information in a team obeya room.

Kyle had a good question for the team. "Some of the NBT project content is sensitive, and it's not supposed to be shared outside of the team. How can we keep this information secure?"

That prompted Adam to jump in. "I can set up the room with special security access so only people with the appropriate permission can enter it."

Krisha wondered out loud. "What about the stakeholders who aren't located in our building?"

Adam offered his assistance again. "I could set up an obeya website designed for our team members and stakeholders that shows the same information that's in the physical obeya room. Of course, the team members and stakeholders would also be have permission to access that website."

Kyle liked both ideas.

JUST IN TIME (JIT)

"This is a concept you might have heard of," Sam told them.

"Just in time, or JIT, is a type of inventory management in which materials, labor, and other needed items are scheduled to arrive at the precise time they are needed. This means there is little or no extra stock held in inventory, which helps companies to lower their inventory carrying costs and decrease waste.

"On a project, subject matter experts are needed at certain times. It would be best to use them just in time, so the project is not waiting for them, nor are they assigned too soon, wasting their time while they wait for their work to begin.

"It's the project manager's responsibility to ensure subject matter experts are appropriately scheduled. As for materials and other needed items, the project manager will work with procurement, supply chain, and other subject matter experts to use JIT management."

STANDARD WORK

"A good way to improve efficiency and to avoid mistakes is by standardizing work methods." Sam waited for a moment while Kyle finished taking notes. Then she continued.

"Standard work methods enable different people to perform repeated tasks in the same way. It involves determining the most efficient way to perform all the steps in a process, documenting those steps, and then performing them repeatedly in the same manner in the future. While assembly lines use robots and other techniques to ensure standard work methods, project-related standard work includes having reliable standardized processes, procedures, and templates."

PLAN-DO-CHECK-ACT

"Plan-Do-Check-Act (PDCA) is the Lean operating framework and a methodology used for implementing kaizen and kaikaku events." Sam approached the markerboard and drew a diagram.

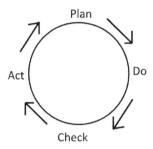

"It is also known as the Deming cycle, the Shewhart cycle, or the Plan–Do–Study–Act (PDSA) cycle.

"The cycle is meant to be short, and the steps can be repetitive." She wrote the on the markerboard:

PDCA

Plan by analyzing and identifying the problem that needs to be solved

Do or develop solutions to analyze

Check or study the effectiveness of the solution and make improvements

Act and implement the revised solution

"Practicing PDCA can help teams identify and validate solutions and improve them. It also promotes productivity and efficiency because it involves commitment to continuous improvement."

Kyle thought about how PDCA parallels the phases in the project management lifecycle: initiating, planning, executing, monitoring and controlling, and closing.

DMAIC

"DMAIC (Define, Measure, Analyze, Improve and Control) is an improvement tool with five interconnected process steps used to drive Six Sigma projects. It's used to improve existing process problems when the cause of the problems is unknown."

Sam wrote on the markerboard:

DMAIC

Define the goal, problem, scope, customer, outputs

Measure baselines, intermediate milestones, final performance

Analyze the root cause of problems, process inputs and outputs

Improve by reducing defects and making the current processes better

Control by embedding changes, tracking improvements, and ensuring sustainability

---

Kyle thought about how the DMAIC cycle also parallels the project management lifecycle. There were a few extra DMAIC items that weren't included in his project management training, including analyzing root causes of problems, embedding changes, and ensuring sustainability.

Sam smiled at the team. "Now let's change our focus for a minute. Why are we working on these projects?" No one looked up.

"Because the customer wants the result of the projects. So we need to include the customer's point of view in the process of creating the product."

VOICE OF THE CUSTOMER

"The Voice of the Customer (VOC) includes the customer's perspective, needs, expectations, preferences, and comments. There are many ways to ensure you have accurately received the voice of the customer, including gathering feedback, holding interviews, and conducting focus groups, surveys, or information gathering meetings."

Kyle recalled how, prior to that Terrible Tuesday, he heard second or thirdhand what the customers were expecting. Sadly, the team often missed the mark, and customers did not get what they expected. He walked to the Terrible Tuesday list on the flip chart to address the fifth item.

5. Problem: customers are not getting what they expect

   Solution: Document the Voice of the Customer (VOC) to get the customer's perspective, needs, expectations, preferences, and comments.

"Are there any other questions?" There were none, so Sam wrapped up the session. "That concludes our learning sessions on Lean."

The team looked a little drained, except for Kyle. He was invigorated by what he learned. He was relieved to have realistic solutions for the items on the Terrible Tuesday list. "I have to admit, there were several topics you covered that I wish I had known about during the last project. I'm eager to apply them to the NBT project, and all other projects going forward. You've done a great job of explaining the Lean world to us."

"I learned quite a bit about project management too," Charles admitted. "I have a whole new respect for it now."

Everyone else nodded in agreement. Sam smiled. "Thank you." She was happy that they appreciated the learning sessions.

SOLUTIONS FOR THE LIST

Kyle was still adding Lean solutions to the Terrible Tuesday list. When he was finished, he had more than one solution for every problem. He reviewed the solutions with the team.

Solutions for the Terrible Tuesday List

1. Time is wasted while trying to solve the wrong problems.
   Solutions:
   - Use the Five Whys to confirm and find the root cause of a problem by asking a sequence of "why" questions at least five times.
   - Complete Gemba walks to fully understand how work is being done. Closely observe the people and the processes and learn from them where the true problems exist.
   - Use the A3 approach to document the root cause of problems and proposed countermeasures.
   - Complete current state value stream maps to see where waste is happening, where problems exist, and where kaizen events/improvements should be made.

2. Projects are disorganized.
   Solutions:
   - Apply 5S (Sort, Set in Order, Shine, Systematize, Standardize.) to make the workplace well organized and productive.
   - Use standard work methods.
   - Be on the lookout for DOWNTIME, the eight forms of waste: defects, over production, waiting, non-utilized

talent, (unnecessary) transportation, (excess) inventory, (wasted) motion, and excess processing.

- Be on the lookout for muda, muri, and mura (wastefulness, unevenness or irregularity, overburden or excessiveness)

3. It takes too long to get decisions made and approved.
   Solutions:
   - Practice nemawashi, the informal process of gaining consensus. Meet with stakeholders to describe proposed changes or decisions needed and gather their support, consensus and decisions BEFORE inviting them to a formal meeting. Turn the meeting into a summary meeting versus a decision-making meeting.
   - Influence decision-makers by walking them through the current state process to see the areas of concern. Also walk them through the future state process to show the positive impact of their decision.

4. Status updates are complicated and confusing.
   Solutions:
   - Use Visual Management, Visual Management Boards, and Visual Control methods (signs, graphics, or other forms of eye-catching displays) to help share/report information in a format that is easier to understand and faster to read.
   - Display the visual information in a team obeya room.

5. Customers are not getting what they expect.
   Solutions:
   - Document the voice of the customer to get the customer's perspective, needs, expectations, preferences, and comments.

- Create value stream maps to determine and show where the value to the customer is.

When Kyle finished his review, Sam addressed the group. "Thank you, everyone, for taking the time to learn about both project management and Lean methods."

She continued in a serious tone. "But just learning about each of them is not enough. We need to integrate the two together and to create a Lean Project Management culture."

The team members nodded in agreement.

Kyle looked at his team members. "As the project manager, I'll need your support with making this happen on the NBT project. Are you in?" The group nodded in agreement. Then he took a risk. He put his right hand in the center of the table where the team members were sitting. In a show of support for the project and in an effort to start team building, he invited others to join him.

Jean-Francois was the first to place his hand on top of Kyle's. Then Adam followed. Then Krisha, Charles and others stacked their hands on top.

"At the count of three … we are NBT!" Kyle counted, "one, two, three" and the team shouted, "We are NBT!"

Kyle reviewed the description of the NBT project with the team, and then, glancing at his notes from the project management learning sessions, he talked about the next steps. "Our first major milestone is to complete the project's Initiating Phase." He reminded the team of what's included in the Initiating Phase.

- Confirm there is an initial Business Case
- Assign a project manager (done)
- Gather historical project information
- Ensure the cultural environment, existing systems and policies are understood
- Define the project goals and create a project charter
- Conduct a formal project Kickoff meeting

While the team reviewed the list, they determined who would gather which information and when the information would be needed.

Jean-Francois had already been working on the initial Business Case. He agreed to get Emma's acceptance of it.

Kyle reminded them, "We'll need to gather any relevant historical data and previous lessons learned — if any were documented — that could be helpful to us. We should also see if there is any existing standard work we can use, like templates, existing processes, procedures, and so on."

Krisha offered her assistance. "I can help gather anything that's software-related, including any previous business requirements."

Adam added, "I can gather previous drawings, schematics diagrams, change notices, bills of materials, and regulatory documents that are in the computer system."

Charles also offered to help. "I can get the manufacturing routings, machine set-ups, and the list of approved suppliers."

Kyle smiled. "Thanks. I'll also need input from each of you as I create the project charter, especially when it comes to creating a schedule, a cost estimate, and a detailed description of what's in scope."

As Kyle finished his requests, the team members started packing up their things.

Then Sam spoke up. "Hold on everyone! It's great that you're all going to work on those things, but I noticed everything mentioned was project management-related. Don't forget to integrate Lean with your project management."

Although they had just learned about Lean, the team members were confused about how to start applying it.

Sam suggested, "Let's talk through this for a minute. We don't want to repeat the mistakes we've made in the past. We want to manage a better project that creates a better product than we have in the past. We want to solve the problems that our past projects have been plagued with."

"That's for sure!" Kyle responded.

Sam continued. "In order to make things better, we need to thoroughly understand how things are done today. One of the best ways to do that is to conduct Gemba walks. We'll get valuable input from the people doing all kinds of work during every step of the project, including how the existing products are being assembled. We could learn from these people about how we should do things differently next time." Sam looked at Kyle.

"Okay, we can conduct Gemba walks," Kyle responded.

Sam continued. "Let's talk more about our existing problems. We have a list of some of our problems, but it would be better if we showed specifically *where* in the process those problems exist. Once we create a value stream map showing the current process, we can highlight the existing problems and areas where improvements should be made. The highlighted problem areas will become future kaizen events.

"Lastly, remember that the project goals, objectives, and the deliverables are all meant to represent the customers' needs and expectations. You'll want to document the VOC."

Kyle thought to himself, *it would be helpful for the team — especially team members who don't get the opportunity to communicate directly with the customer — to see for themselves specifically what the customer is requesting.* He remembered that this too was a remedy for the Terrible Tuesday list.

He agreed. "Okay, we'll add a section called Voice of the Customer."

Sam continued, "We just covered several items, so I'll summarize them here."

She wrote on the markerboard.

1. Conduct Gemba walks to observe and better understand the current problems and processes.
2. Create a current state value stream map.
3. On the map, highlight existing problems and areas where improvements should be made.

4. Document the root causes of the problems.
5. Document the voice of the customer.

Kyle was a little confused. "I guess that all makes sense. But if we're going to do all this, shouldn't we also be completing kaizen events and creating a future state value stream map?"

"Great question!" Sam responded with an enthusiastic smile. "Yes, we need to do those things too, but we can do them in the Planning Phase. To create a good project charter, we at least need to have a thorough understanding of the current problems and processes, and we *must* have a clear understanding of what the customer wants, needs, and expects. Otherwise we would all be working on a project where we are trying to address problems and fix processes we don't fully understand, and we would risk delivering something other than what the customer expects."

Suddenly, a light bulb came on in Kyle's mind. "We definitely don't want to address the wrong problems, and we don't want to have any team members disagreeing on or misunderstanding what the current problems are. That would result in significant waste. And absolutely, we want the customer to be happy and to get what they expect."

Sam smiled. "I think you've got it."

Section 4

LEAN PROJECT MANAGEMENT IN ACTION

Initiating a Project

Kyle was eager to get the project charter started. "Before you spend significant time on the charter, you should make sure an initial Business Case has been completed," Sam advised.

A Business Case had been drafted specifically for the NTB project by Jean-Francois with input from the Accounting department, and then it was reviewed by Emma. It showed the estimated return on investment for the NBT project. It was aligned with the general goals of The Flying Machine, Inc., and it provided the financial justification to work on the project. Kyle reviewed it and found the goals listed in it to be realistic and acceptable.

Over the next two weeks, Kyle led the team as they prepared to create a project charter that aligned with the Business Case.

GEMBA WALKS

For the first time, the team conducted Gemba walks. They talked with sales and marketing employees, procurement and supply chain employees, designers, engineers, business analysts and programmers. They arranged with the factory floor supervisors to walk through and observe the current assembly lines and every step of the process required to create and then store new products in the warehouse.

They observed as factory workers struggled to pull molded parts out of presses. They witnessed the workers spending extra time re-working the shapes of metal that didn't arrive from the supplier as expected. They watched with amazement as the workers were careful not to damage anything while trying to stuff the assembled product into a tightly form-fitting box, like trying to fit two pounds of sausage into a casing that only holds one pound. They observed technicians testing products according to complicated test plans. They even watched as forklifts carefully loaded packaged products into large trucks.

The team asked questions and took careful notes as they learned what it's like to actually produce the products they designed. It was an eye-opening experience for the entire team, and it gave them a much greater appreciation for the people doing the factory work.

VALUE STREAM MAPPING

After the Gemba walks, the team created a value stream map of the current state of the process they had been using to do deliver value to the customer. They wrote each step of the process on a large index card and taped it to the wall so it could easily be moved if someone thought of an additional step that should go before or after it.

The map spanned the length of the conference room and even wrapped around a corner. It provided a visual baseline of the existing process steps and the value being delivered. It showed the flow of each step from beginning to end, including the tools and systems used, people involved, approvals required, and decision points.

The team was engaged and enjoyed making the map. They even took pictures of it. When it was completed, the team stepped back and looked at it in amazement. Kyle was impressed. "There's an awful lot going on here! I always knew what my part of the process was, but now I can see *everyone's part*."

HIGHLIGHTING EXISTING PROBLEMS

They highlighted problem areas, including steps in the process that the customer would not value, where time was being wasted, where too many people were working on a task, and where too much risk was being taken.

DOCUMENTING ROOT CAUSES

For each problem area, they had fun asking each other the Five Whys to help them get to the root cause. For some problems, it wasn't easy to determine the root cause, so in those cases, specific team members were assigned to complete a one-page A3 document.

DOCUMENTING THE VOICE OF THE CUSTOMER

Later that week, Jean-Francois invited Kyle to travel with him and meet with a few key customers to discuss the NBT project. During the meetings Kyle listened closely to the customers, documenting the NBT project's value from their perspective. He learned directly from them what they needed and what they expected.

After the meetings Kyle shared the customers' feedback with the team, and together they agreed on the most important VOC bullet points to add to the project charter.

After spending time completing this work with the team, both Sam and Kyle felt comfortable with the contents of the project charter. Kyle thought that the deliverables, schedule, and cost estimates were all more accurate than in the past, thanks to the findings from their recently conducted Gemba walks and value stream maps.

The team had a much better understanding of the problems that existed within The Flying Machine's current state processes. They felt confident that their understanding of the root causes would help them create a much better product going forward.

When Kyle compiled all the information into the project charter, it included:

- the goals of the project
- the objectives
- the deliverables
- a list of what was in scope and what was not in scope
- a list of high-level risks
- a list of assumptions
- a cost estimate for the project
- the completion date
- the acceptance criteria
- a list of the most relevant stakeholders
- the name of the project sponsor (Eamon)
- the name of the project manager (Kyle)
- a section called Known Problems and Their Root Causes, and
- a section for the Voice of the Customer.

The entire charter fit on a two-sided piece of paper. It was to-the-point and could be read in a minute. Kyle was proud of it.

APPROVAL AND PREPARATION FOR KICKOFF

That Friday, Kyle reviewed the project charter with Sam.

"Great work, Kyle."

"Thanks, Sam. It took longer than usual to create it, but it's much more accurate and realistic than past charters. And now that I've done it the first time, it will be easier in the future."

Together, they reviewed the charter with Eamon. After a brief discussion, Eamon formally approved it by signing and dating it. He was impressed with the work that went into making it a credible document, especially since The Flying Machine had a history of charters that were rushed, vague and unrealistic.

Kyle sent a Kickoff Meeting invitation to the stakeholders. He planned to review the project charter with them and was hopeful that everyone would agree with it. This was an important meeting. Everything had been going well so far on the project, and he wanted to keep that momentum.

Soon after, Sam stopped by Kyle's office. "Do you have a minute?" she asked.

"Sure."

"I have two recommendations for you that will increase the odds of accomplishing a successful Kickoff Meeting."

"Sounds great. I'm all ears."

Sam explained. "First, I recommend that you practice nemawashi. Meet with each stakeholder separately and get their buy-in on the project charter *before* they come to the Kickoff Meeting. The last thing you want is for stakeholders to disagree with the charter *during* the meeting."

He like the idea but was concerned. "It's going to take a significant amount of time to meet with people prior to the Kickoff Meeting."

Sam insisted. "Trust me on this one. It will be worth your time, and you'll be amazed at the results. Be sure to meet with the key (or highest priority) stakeholders, and if there's time you can meet with additional stakeholders. Review the charter with them and answer any questions they have. Then ask them if you have their support for the project."

She continued. "Second, ask Emma if she would come to the beginning of the Kickoff Meeting to offer some words of encouragement to the team and the stakeholders."

Kyle looked uncomfortable. "She's the CEO! I can't ask her to attend my meeting!"

Sam smiled and continued. "Sure you can. It's a great way to let the group know how important this project is!"

He reluctantly agreed to talk to Emma.

After Sam met with Kyle, she met with Emma to give her some advanced notice. "Remember when you asked me to let you know when you could help? It would be a great start for the NBT project if you came to the Kickoff Meeting to show your support for the team and the stakeholders. Would you mind doing that?"

Emma didn't have to think about it. "Just tell me when and where and I'll be there." Sam explained to Emma that she would receive an invitation soon from Kyle.

So, Kyle asked Emma to attend the meeting. When she quickly agreed, he was flabbergasted, but excited.

Then, after sending Emma and the other stakeholders an advance copy of the project charter, he met individually with each of them to review it.

After the stakeholders received answers to their various questions, Kyle courageously asked, "Do I have your support for the project?" Each stakeholder promised him their support. During each discussion, he got to know the stakeholders a little better, and he felt more confident about the upcoming Kickoff Meeting.

The day before the Kickoff Meeting, Sam coached Kyle on how to present the project charter that he and the team had prepared.

THE KICKOFF MEETING

On the morning of the meeting, Kyle was well prepared. "Welcome to the NBT project!" he said, as everyone settled in their seats and all the remote stakeholders logged into the video conference.

Sam, Eamon, and Emma were there too.

Emma spoke to the team for a few minutes about the importance of the NBT project to The Flying Machine. "Each of you plays a key role in making the project a success. Launching our new microprocessor technology will send a message to our customers that The Flying Machine is the drone company of the future. Keeping to the committed schedule will position us to beat Tornado to the market. Keeping to the committed cost will increase value for our customers, keep the price reasonable, and allow us to reach our sales and profit goals." She thanked everyone in advance for their hard work and commitment.

Kyle already felt Sam's support, and now he felt supported by Emma also. His confidence was increasing every day.

Next, Jean-Francois provided everyone with an overview of the Business Case. Then Kyle reviewed the project charter with the group and answered their questions. He explained how the project team was practicing Lean Project Management and that they had recently attended learning sessions on both Lean and project management principles. The stakeholders had already heard about the recent learning sessions and were pleased to see that the team was taking action to overcome the many previous problems at The Flying Machine. The stakeholders were also impressed by the team's work so far. It had resulted in a credible, concise, and organized charter document.

Kyle thanked everyone who had provided their input into the charter. Then he talked briefly about the importance of revisiting the Business Case from time to time. "At milestone checkpoints we'll compare our project status to both the Business Case goals and the expected customer value to ensure that the project is still moving in the intended direction. We'll confirm that the reasons for working on the project still exist."

Then he talked about what would be coming next. "Next, we'll enter the Planning Phase of the project." He referred to his presentation. "In the coming weeks, the team will work together to create important assessments, plans, and estimates that we'll need during the project. He showed them what would be included in the Project Management Plan.

Project Management Plan:

Detailed Project Schedule
Defined Team Roles and Responsibilities
Detailed Cost Estimate
Stakeholder Assessment
Communication Plan
Risk Assessment
Procurement Plan
Quality Plan
Scope Change Control Plan

The Kickoff Meeting lasted for about 30 minutes. Because Kyle had received buy-in from the stakeholders prior to the meeting, there were no concerns and only a few questions. At the end of the meeting, everyone in the room and those logged into the video conference applauded! It was, by far, the most uplifting and successful Kickoff Meeting Kyle and the team had experienced.

After the meeting, Kyle thought about the extra time the team had taken to apply Lean principles while creating the project charter and while preparing for the Kickoff Meeting. That preparation had taken a little longer than on previous projects, but it saved them a significant amount of time overall. Kyle would not have to defend a weak charter, and he wouldn't have to waste time resolving disagreements and confusion after the Kickoff Meeting.

Spending a little extra time upfront using Lean methods would save a significant amount of time later. And this was just the beginning.

DOCUMENTING THE LESSONS LEARNED

After the Kickoff Meeting, Sam advised Kyle to spend some time thinking about the lessons he had learned about Lean Project Management. She also coached him on how to involve the team to capture their lessons learned.

The next day, Kyle gathered the team. "Let's document what we've learned during the Initiating Phase. Keep in mind that that capturing the lessons we've learned is not about blaming anyone. It's about practicing continuous improvement. It's about making things easier for us going forward and for the next team assigned to a similar project."

So the team documented what worked well and what they recommended doing differently on future projects.

Next, they talked about how best to prepare as they entered the Planning Phase.

"We need that obeya room we learned about," Krisha commented.

Kyle responded. "You're right. We've already created super valuable information that the team and the stakeholders will need to refer to on a regular basis. It should all be on display in an obeya room."

That afternoon, Sam was able to reserve a room for Kyle that could serve as the NBT obeya room throughout the life of the project. At this point, Kyle was able to display hard copies of the current state value stream map and the charter.

With Adam's assistance, Kyle arranged to have a phone and video conferencing equipment set up in the room so it could be used for future team and stakeholder meetings.

To help any off-site stakeholders see the same documents that were displayed in the obeya room, Adam created a secure obeya website displaying electronic versions of the documents.

For more detailed documents that only the immediate team needed to use and share with each other, Adam set up a secure, shared team website. Adam shared the websites with the team, as well as the procedures for organizing files and for document version control.

Kyle stored the Lessons Learned document in the shared team site. He encouraged the team to continue adding lessons they learned to it at any time throughout the project.

HOW TO MAKE IT LEAN

After the team finished documenting all the lessons they had learned so far, they talked about the benefits of applying Lean principles.

Krisha shared her thoughts. "I feel confident that we're addressing the right problems because we created a current state Value Stream Map of our existing process that pinpoints exactly what needs to be addressed and where we are spending extra time on tasks that don't provide value to our customers."

"And we're *not* chasing after problems just because they were raised by the loudest opinion in the room." Eamon added, trying hard not to glance over at Charles. "And we learned from the Gemba walks how work is really being done today instead of second-guessing how it's done."

Kyle added his opinion. "Speaking of second-guessing, now that we've documented the actual Voice of the Customer, we have no questions about what our customers' expectations are. Also, practicing nemawashi to gather stakeholders' consensus on the charter *before* presenting it at the Kickoff Meeting resulted in an organized and efficient meeting." The rest of the team nodded in agreement.

They wrapped up with a discussion about how they could create standard work that would help future Flying Machine projects to be Lean. They decided to create a table showing the project management activities needed for the Initiating Phase and the corresponding Lean activities.

How to Make the Initiating Phase Lean

Project Management Activity	How to Make It Lean
Confirm there is an initial Business Case that aligns the project with the company's organizational goals.	Gather or create a current state Value Stream Map showing the existing value to the customer. Obtain the Voice of the Customer and document their expectations for the project.
Assign a project manager.	Provide Lean training for the project manager.
Gather historical project information and lessons learned from similar projects.	Conduct a Gemba walk to observe how work is currently being completed. Get input from the people doing the work about how the existing organization operates and its history. See what standard work already exists and can be used for this project.

Project Management Activity	How to Make It Lean
Identify and document the root causes of problems that the project will address.	Ask the Five Whys. Apply the "A" from DMAIC by analyzing root causes. Create A3's to help identify problems and their root causes. On the current state value stream maps, highlight areas that need to be improved.
Understand the cultural environment, existing systems, policies.	Conduct Gemba walks to observe the cultural climate. Discover which processes and systems are helpful, and what policies and procedures exist.

Project Management Activity	How to Make It Lean
Define goals and create a project charter.	Apply the "D" from DMAIC by defining the goal, problem, scope, customer(s), deliverables. Apply the "M" from DMAIC by measuring current scenarios so you have something to compare and show improvements against later. Plan to deliver only what the customer values, and to let the customer pull what is expected.
Conduct a formal Kick-off Meeting.	Conduct nemawashi to gain stakeholder consensus on the project charter before holding the Kickoff Meeting.

Planning a Project

The following Monday, Sam and Kyle met to discuss the Planning Phase. They agreed that Sam would provide coaching for the team at the beginning of each topic, and then Kyle would take the lead on completing the work — with input from the team. To get the team thinking about what was coming, prior to the Planning meeting Kyle sent them a reminder of everything that's included in a project management plan.

Project Management Plan

Detailed Project Schedule
Defined Team Roles and Responsibilities
Detailed Cost Estimate
Stakeholder Assessment
Communication Plan
Risk Assessment
Procurement Plan
Quality Plan
Scope Change Control Plan

The next day, the team gathered to begin the Planning Phase.

Sam greeted them. "Welcome to the Planning Phase. As you know, the NBT charter document has been formally approved. It contains all the information necessary to start the project and to help guide the team through executing the project.

"So far, at a high level, we've defined *what* is required to complete the project. The Planning Phase is where we define *how* to complete the project. Kyle sent you a list of what goes into a project management plan."

DETAILED PROJECT SCHEDULE

"We'll start by creating a detailed project schedule. In order to do that, we're going to need a work breakdown structure."

Krisha spoke up. "We learned that we should use standard work where possible, so we looked for an existing work breakdown structure that we could refer to and then revise as needed, but we couldn't find one."

Sam was happy to hear that Krisha was thinking about standard work. "I'm glad you took the time to see if standard work exists," she said. "No worries, we'll start by listing some major categories of work." She passed out large index cards and markers. "We'll write one category of work on each card."

After a few minutes of discussion, the team members agreed on the categories: Project Management, Marketing & Design, Engineering, Procurement & Supply Chain, Manufacturing, Final Testing, and Approvals. They taped each card to the wall. Then they listed the work that needed to take place within each category on smaller index cards. As they continued, it started to look like this.

NBT Work Breakdown Structure (WBS)

NBT Project

Project Management
- Project Schedule
- Project Budget
- Communication Plan
- Scope Change Approval Process
- Risk Management Plan
- Stakeholder Management Plan
- Confirm Roles and Responsibilities
- Quality Plan
- Status Updates
  - Internal
  - Customer

Marketing & Design
- Market Research
  - Focus Group Testing
- Marketing Plan
- Commercialization Plan
- Renderings
- Models

Engineering
- Mechanical Design/CAD
- Patent Applications
- Packaging Design
- Tooling Design
- Prototyping
- Bills of Materials
- User & Service Instructions
- Electronic Eng & Progr
  - Circuit Board Design
  - Programming
  - Coding
  - Testing

Procurement & Supply Chain
- Supplier Qualifications
- Confidentiality Agreements
- RFPs/SOWs
- Supplier Bidding
- Purchase Orders
- Contracts
- Vendor Management
- Inventory Management

Manufacturing
- Routings
- Assembly Line Layouts
- Training of Workers
- Mfg & Assembly
- Quality Control Inspections
- Warehousing
- Shipping

Final Testing
- Component Testing
- Vehicle Testing
- Controller Testing
- Transit Testing
- Regulatory Testing

Approvals
- Internal Approvals
- Customer Approvals
- Gov't Approvals

They all took a step back and looked at the entire WBS in amazement, realizing how much they had just accomplished. Adam took a picture of it. "It's so interesting to see the big picture showing everything that needs to be done!"

Kyle nodded in agreement. "If we hadn't gone through this exercise together, I wouldn't know all the work to account for in the project schedule."

Sam suggested, "Let's take a few minutes to discuss how long the work will take and the order in which the work should be completed."

Over the next hour the team rearranged the index cards according to the phases in the lifecycle of a project. They showed what needed to happen first, then what came next, and so on. They showed which tasks could take place in parallel with other tasks and which tasks had to wait for others to finish before they could start. Each task had a duration written on it to show about how long it should take to complete it. When they were finished, they had a Gantt chart made from index cards that took up the whole wall.

Charles spoke up. "This was such a helpful exercise. I also like how I can see all the work needed to complete the project – all on one page. Anyone could read this in less than a minute! That's Lean."

After the session, Sam and Kyle talked about what had just happened.

She explained, "When team members work together to create the WBS, team building takes place. Each person provides their input and expertise, and when they're finished, they each walk away feeling that their experience and opinions have been heard and valued."

"Free team building. That's clever!" Kyle responded.

After Kyle received input from the team on the estimated durations and the logical sequence for each of the tasks listed in the WBS, he entered the information into his project scheduling software to create a detailed schedule. The schedule showed the task names, the start and finish dates, and the chronological order of each of the tasks. It showed which tasks could be worked on in parallel with other tasks and which ones could not begin until other tasks were completed.

The schedule even included the project management-related tasks and the major steps within the Flying Machine's Product Development Process. When Kyle was finished, the schedule showed the entire project from start to finish. But this was just a draft. He needed to review it with the team.

After reviewing the schedule with the team and everyone giving their input, Charles spoke up. "For the first time I can actually *read* a project schedule — and it makes sense to me!"

"What do you mean?" Kyle was puzzled.

Charles explained what he meant. "In the past, I've been asked to review schedules that were long and confusing. I'd fall asleep halfway through them. Now that I've provided input into the work breakdown structure, I can see how the schedule was created. I helped create it! That process makes it so much easier to understand. You actually have my buy-in." The rest of the team agreed.

NBT Detailed Project Schedule
(In Process)

Task Name	Duration	Start	Finish	January	February	March
NBT Project	280 days	Jan 2	Jan 27			
Initiating	46 days	Jan 2	Mar 5			
Confirm there is an initial Business Case	3 days	Jan 2	Jan 6			
Product Development Process Phase 1: Research	3 wks	Jan 7	Jan 27			
Gather historical project information and lessons learned	1 wk	Jan 28	Feb 3			
Document the root causes of problems the project will address	2 wks	Feb 4	Feb 17			
Define goals and create a Project Charter	2 wks	Feb 18	Mar 2			
Conduct a formal Kickoff Meeting	1 day	Mar 3	Mar 3			
Document the lessons learned	2 days	Mar 4	Mar 5			
Planning	17 days	Mar 6	Mar 30			
Finalize the Project Management Plan	17 days	Mar 6	Mar 30			
Create a Work Breakdown Structure	1 wk	Mar 6	Mar 12			
Create a Project Schedule	1 wk	Mar 13	Mar 19			
Aquire Resources	2 wks	Mar 6	Mar 19			
Confirm Roles and Responsibilities	2 wks	Mar 6	Mar 19			
Complete a detailed Cost Estimate	1 wk	Mar 6	Mar 12			
Complete a Stakeholder Assessment	2 days	Mar 6	Mar 9			
Complete a Communication Plan	2 days	Mar 6	Mar 9			
Conduct a Risk Assessment	3 days	Mar 6	Mar 10			
Complete a Procurement Plan	2 days	Mar 6	Mar 9			
Confirm the Scope Management Plan	2 days	Mar 6	Mar 9			
Complete a Quality Management Plan	2 days	Mar 6	Mar 9			
Product Development Process Phase 2: Concept	2 wks	Mar 10	Mar 23			
Document the lessons learned	1 wk	Mar 24	Mar 30			
Executing	165 days	Jun 4	Jan 20			
Product Development Process Phase 3: Analyze	165 days	Jun 4	Jan 20			

148

Sam was pleased that the team liked participating in creating the schedule.

Kyle added, "We'll need to make some adjustments to the schedule as we complete the rest of our project plan. For example, once we agree on roles and responsibilities, I can add names to each of the tasks in the schedule."

Sam nodded in agreement. "Also, keep in mind that once the team completes a risk assessment, you'll need to adjust the plan based on whatever risk mitigation plans the team decides on. You'll also need to add any planned kaizen or kaikaku events.

"After that, you'll be able to call the schedule the *baseline* schedule. Going forward, you'll use it to compare your original plan — your baseline — to your actual progress."

Charles thought to himself, I *don't recall learning how to create project schedules in my Lean training.* But he was pleased with what he saw and felt good since he and the team participated in making it. The entire schedule could be reviewed by anyone in less than a minute.

Kyle displayed the draft schedule in the obeya room and on the obeya website.

TEAM ROLES AND RESPONSIBILITIES

Kyle and the team referred to the WBS and the schedule to see which work the existing team members could complete and which work required additional resources. They talked about who was best suited to complete the work and discussed work that would require them to look outside the company for temporary contract help.

Sam pointed out, "You'll need to instill a team culture of Lean Project Management."

The team members all nodded in agreement. She continued, "New team members will look to each of you for guidance and to set examples. What you do, and how you act, sets the Lean Project Management culture for the whole team — and possibly the whole company. You should each feel empowered to point out waste and any scenarios where it looks like customers aren't getting the value promised to them. In other words, you'll need to *put into practice* what you've learned if you want it to work."

Kyle added, "We'll continue to hold our team meetings in the obeya room so everyone can easily see our charter, WBS, schedule, and more. The obeya room, as well as the obeya website, will be available to the team and stakeholders at all times."

Sam added, "You could also focus on 5S with regard to your workspaces, obeya room, workshop, staging and storage areas, and even your electronic storage of team documents. That means Sort, Set in Order, Shine, Systematize, and Standardize."

Jean-Francois, whose office was the messiest of all, even committed to cleaning and organizing it that afternoon.

Adam reminded the team about keeping their electronic documents organized and stored within the team site.

Krisha was curious. "Should we train our incoming team members on Lean and project management?"

Sam liked her idea and replied, "You bet! I can help with that."

Glancing at the major tasks shown in the schedule, and the WBS, Sam advised the team. "As you work together to assign roles and responsibilities for each task, you'll need to create a RACI chart." Then she shared the following descriptions with the team.

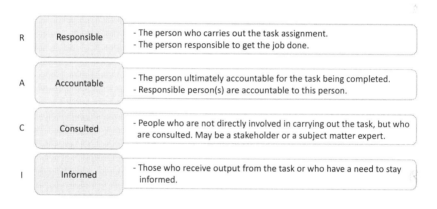

R	Responsible	- The person who carries out the task assignment. - The person responsible to get the job done.
A	Accountable	- The person ultimately accountable for the task being completed. - Responsible person(s) are accountable to this person.
C	Consulted	- People who are not directly involved in carrying out the task, but who are consulted. May be a stakeholder or a subject matter expert.
I	Informed	- Those who receive output from the task or who have a need to stay informed.

"For each major task, document who should be listed as the person *responsible* for completing the task by assigning an R beside their name. Then document who should be *accountable* by assigning an 'A' to their name. The next step is to document who should be consulted with – by assigning a 'C'. Lastly, document who should be kept *informed* by assigning an 'I'."

The project schedule already listed all the major tasks, so instead of taking extra time to create a new document with much of the same information on it, Kyle added columns to the existing project schedule. He added the team members' names and roles at the top. The RACI chart was taking shape and started to look like this.

NBT RACI Chart
(In Process)

Task Name	Kyle (Project Mgmt)	Krisha (Engr/Progr)	Charles (Manufacturing)	Jean-Francois (Sales & Mktg)	Adam (IT)	Eamon (Sponsor)
⊿ NBT Project						
⊿ Initiating						
Confirm there is an Initial Business Case	A		I	R	I	C
Product Development Process Phase 1: Research	A	I	I	I	I	R
Gather historical project information and lessons learned	A/R	C	C	C	C	C
Document the root causes of problems the project will address	A/R	C	C	C	C	C
Define goals and create a Project Charter	A/R	C	C	C	C	C
Conduct a formal Kickoff Meeting	A/R	C	C	C	C	C
Document the lessons learned	A/R	C	C	C	C	C
⊿ Planning						
⊿ Finalize the Project Management Plan	A/R	C	C	C	C	C
Create a Work Breakdown Structure	A/R	C	C	C	C	C
Create a Project Schedule	A/R					
Aquire Resources	A/R	C	C	C	C	C
Confirm Roles and Responsibilities	A/R	C	C	C	C	C
Complete a detailed Cost Estimate	A/R	C	C	C	C	C
Complete a Stakeholder Assessment	A/R	C	C	C	C	C
Complete a Communication Plan	A/R	C	C	C	C	C
Conduct a Risk Assessment	A/R	C	C	C	C	C
Complete a Procurement Plan	A/R	C	C	C	C	C
Confirm the Scope Management Plan	A/R	C	C	C	C	C
Complete a Quality Management Plan	A/R	C	C	C	C	C
Product Development Process Phase 2: Concept	A	I	I	R	I	I
Document the lessons learned	A/R	C	C	C	C	C
⊿ Executing						
⊿ Product Development Process Phase 3: Analyze	A	C				

Charles offered his feedback. "This was another helpful exercise for me. It's amazing how I can see all the work needed to complete the project and who's assigned to get it done – all on one page. Anyone could read this in less than a minute! That's Lean!"

Looking at Kyle, Sam reminded them, "To reduce waste, you'll need to properly leverage the subject matter expert's skills. Apply Just in Time (JIT) workload assignments to prevent team members from waiting around for their work to begin or from attending meetings where they aren't needed. Applying JIT will also prevent bottlenecks due to team members being overloaded." Kyle nodded in agreement.

Team members recommended a few people for specific tasks who were not present during the RACI exercise. After the meeting, Kyle spent some time talking with department leaders to see if the people who had been recommended could be made available to take on that work. Once he got agreement from the department leaders, he spent time with each newly assigned person to explain the goals of the project. He gave them a description of their role. Kyle also provided them with access to the obeya room, the obeya website, and the shared team site, and he gave them a copy of the project schedule and the RACI chart. He also invited them to attend future learning sessions on Lean Project Management.

In the project schedule, he added each new person's name to the specific tasks they would perform. Since the schedule showed the estimated duration of each task, it was easy to see how much of each person's time would be needed to complete the assigned tasks. Team members could even tell when they were scheduled to start each task and the targeted finish date.

PROJECT COST ESTIMATE

The next day, in the NBT obeya room, Sam and Kyle revisited the cost estimate documented in the project's charter document.

Sam explained, "The cost estimate in the Charter was based on assumptions and the information the team had at that time. Now you'll need to get into the details and create a more accurate estimate. You'll need to reference the information in the WBS and the project schedule. And of course, you'll need to get input from the team."

That afternoon, Kyle gathered team members' input on the estimated amount of project spending as well as the estimated timing of when the spending would occur. The estimate summarized the costs of the following items.

- Labor
- Travel expenses
- Consulting and contracting services
- Training
- Testing
- Materials specifically purchased for the NBT project
- Equipment specifically purchased for the NBT project
- Facility upgrades made specifically for the NBT project
- Systems, software, and software licenses specifically for the NBT project

The labor estimate included the SME's time spent on project tasks multiplied by a standard hourly rate. Since the costs were based on information from the detailed schedule, the estimate showed specific timeframes when money would be spent.

The estimate was much more detailed now, and the total was just below the estimate documented in the charter, so Kyle would need to closely monitor spending to make sure it stayed under that amount. If, for some reason (early in the project) he realized that more money would be required to complete the project, he could proactively request additional funding. If that happened, it would be considered a scope change. Also, the Business Case would also need to be recalculated based on the potential increased spending, and the project would need to be re-justified.

"Our estimate is tight," Kyle warned the team. "We'll need to keep an eye out for wastes like muda, mura and muri, and we need to pay attention to DOWNTIME wastes."

Charles gave him a skeptical look. "Do you even remember what DOWNTIME stands for?"

Kyle slowly responded. "Defects, over production, waiting, non-utilized talent, (unnecessary) transportation, (excess) inventory, (wasted) motion, and excess processing or doing more work than necessary."

Jaws dropped as the team members looked at Kyle with amazement. Sam kept a straight face, but she was delighted with Kyle's sincere commitment to understanding Lean.

Once the team reached agreement on the project cost estimate, they kept a copy of it on display in the NBT's obeya room and on the obeya website. The estimated total cost and the actual spending to-date were always shown in comparison to the maximum allowable cost documented in the project charter.

STAKEHOLDER MANAGEMENT

The next day, Sam led the group through a series of Stakeholder Assessments. "When the charter was created, you included a high-level list of stakeholders based on what was known at the time. Now it's time to dig deeper and identify all the stakeholders and what they expect from the project."

She passed around a small stack of sticky notepapers to each team member. "Our goal is to list *all t*he stakeholders by writing each stakeholder's name on a separate paper."

Each team member listed everyone they could think of who was positively or negatively impacted by the project, each on a separate sticky note.

Sam explained, "Some stakeholders have more influence than others. By influence, I mean the ability a stakeholder has to stop or change the project. You'll want to keep these stakeholders satisfied, and some of them you'll want to manage closely.

"And some stakeholders are more interested than others. You'll need to understand the stakeholders' interest levels, so you know how best to keep them informed.

"Let's take a few minutes to consider how much influence and interest our key stakeholders have. To accomplish that, let's see where they fall within the Influence versus Interest grid." Then she taped a poster to the wall.

Stakeholder Influence versus Interest

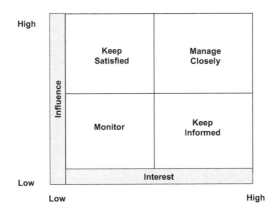

Taking turns, each team member approached the poster with the name of a stakeholder on their sticky notes. Thinking of the level of influence and interest the stakeholder appeared to have, they placed the name of the stakeholder in the most appropriate box. The rest of the team offered their input on the placement. There were some occasions when more than one team member listed the same stakeholder. In those cases, they only stuck the name on the poster once. When they were finished, the poster was filled with names of stakeholders, each in a quadrant, depending on the team's overall perception of their level of influence and interest in the project.

As Sam expected, the names placed in the upper quadrants were people in leadership positions at The Flying Machine. Emma was the president of the company and Eamon, Max, Juan, and Kris were directors.

When the team was finished, the poster looked like this.

NBT Stakeholder Influence versus Interest

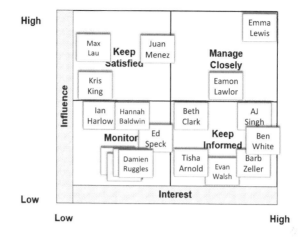

Sam explained, "Now we can see that the stakeholders listed in the upper quadrants have significant influence. But do they have the appropriate amount of interest?" Some have seemingly little interest according to where you placed their names on the grid. Let's take a closer look at the current engagement level of those high influence stakeholders."

CURRENT VERSUS DESIRED ENGAGEMENT LEVEL MATRIX

Sam hung another poster on the wall showing a Current versus Desired Engagement Level matrix. The team discussed each high influence stakeholder and reached a consensus on their current engagement level.

NBT Current versus Desired Engagement Matrix
(Current State)

Stakeholder	Unaware	Resistant	Neutral	Supportive	Leading
Emma Lewis				C	
Eamon Lawlor				C	
Max Lau	C				
Juan Menez		C			
Kris King	C				

C = Current Engagement Level

"Now let me ask you," she said. "Do you think we can be successful if these stakeholders stay at their current engagement level?"

"No!" Most of the team shouted in unison. Kyle was the most concerned. "We definitely won't be successful if we have key stakeholders who are unaware or resistant."

Sam quizzed them. "Where is a reasonable place for each of them to be on this grid?" They discussed each of the stakeholders for a few minutes and arrived at a consensus.

- Emma was *supportive. That was acceptable to the team.*

- Eamon was *supportive,* but as the sponsor they needed him to be in more of a leading role. Not by leading the project, but by showing consistent and visible support for the project, by serving as the escalation path, by approving any scope changes, and more.

- Max from Human Resources was unaware. They needed him to be at least *supportive.*

- Juan from Supply Chain was *resistant,* mostly because he was responsible for inventory reduction and the new project would likely require new inventory. They needed him to be at least *supportive.*

- Kris from the legal department was *unaware.* They needed her to be at least *supportive.*

NBT Current versus Desired Engagement Matrix (Desired State)

Stakeholder	Unaware	Resistant	Neutral	Supportive	Leading
Emma Lewis				C, **D**	
Eamon Lawlor				C	**D**
Max Lau	C			**D**	
Juan Menez		C		**D**	
Kris King	C		**D**		

C = Current Engagement Level
D = Desired Engagement Level

"Now we know the level of engagement we need from our most influential stakeholders. We'll talk soon about how best to communicate with them and influence them so we can move them to the desired state," Sam explained.

"Due to the sensitive nature of these two charts, I recommend keeping this information only within the immediate team, and I don't recommend displaying the charts anywhere."

Kyle agreed. "I'll keep them in my desk drawer for future reference."

STAKEHOLDER EXPECTATIONS

"Next, let's complete the most important stakeholder exercise – Stakeholder Expectations and Success Criteria. It's critical to know what our key stakeholders expect from this project."

She taped a third poster on the wall and added the stakeholders' names on it. "For now, let's document what the 'high influence/ high interest' stakeholders are expecting from the project and what *they* would call a success."

Stakeholder Expectations and Success Criteria

Stakeholder	Expectations and Success Criteria
Emma Lewis	
Eamon Lawlor	
Max Lau	
Juan Menez	
Kris King	

The team spent the next few minutes coming to a consensus on and documenting what they believed the stakeholders expected. When they were finished, their documented Stakeholder Expectations chart looked like this.

NBT Stakeholder Expectations and Success Criteria

Stakeholder	Expectations and Success Criteria
Emma Lewis	• Deliver the value the customer is expecting. • Periodically check to ensure the project is still aligned with the Business Case goals. • Keep leadership informed of high-level risks and issues.
Eamon Lawlor	• Meet cost and delivery targets. • Develop a formal scope control process. • Look for ways to reduce or eliminate waste and to apply continuous improvement.
Max Lau	• Involve the Human Resources department with enlisting external contractors or consultants. • Keep the Human Resources department informed if incentives or overtime pay are needed.
Juan Menez	• Involve the Procurement group and the Supply Chain group in the use of all new suppliers, materials and component parts. • Involve the procurement with the creation of contracts and statements of work.

Stakeholder	Expectations and Success Criteria
Kris King	• Conform to safety requirements. • Involve the legal department in patent searches, patent applications, formal contracts, non-disclosure and confidentiality agreements.

Sam wrapped up the discussion. "Kyle, you will need to visit each of the stakeholders and confirm their expectations. If they aren't completely sure of their expectations yet, invite them to review the Charter again with you. You could also ask them to join the team in some upcoming huddles, Gemba walks, kaizen and kaikaku events.

"If they suggest any adjustments to what we have documented, you'll need to update the document so there is an accurate record. When it's finalized, it will be your official, *internal* Voice of the Customer, or VOC."

"At the risk of sounding like a broken record..." Charles had to speak up. "I like how I can see all of the stakeholders and everything they expect – all on one page. Anyone could read this in less than a minute. That's Lean!"

Sam smiled. "Yes, you sound like a broken record Charles, but it's all good stuff and it's Lean! Thanks for pointing it out." Charles grinned.

Sam continued. "Now that we know how engaged we need our key stakeholders to be and what they expect from our project, we can proactively plan how we will communicate with them to get and keep them engaged. Next we'll will talk about communication management and create a Communication Plan."

COMMUNICATION PLAN

The next day, Sam explained that "Communication management includes knowing who to communicate with, what to communicate, when and how often to communicate, and the best methods to use for communicating." She turned to the markerboard and began writing.

Who — which stakeholders?
What – what is the message?
How (medium) – what's the best way to communicate?
When – when should this be communicated?
How often – what's the frequency for communicating with this
    stakeholder?

"A communication plan will help you organize this information." Then she taped a large poster to the wall and added the high influence stakeholders' names.

Communication Plan

Audience	Message	Medium	Frequency	Timing	Responsibility
Emma Lewis					
Eamon Lawlor					
Max Lau					
Juan Menez					
Kris King					

"It's also important for the team to agree on who is responsible for delivering a particular communication," she explained as she pointed to the 'Responsibility' column.

"You will need to communicate with other people in addition to these key stakeholders." Then she added *Customers* and *All Stakeholders* to the audience column.

Charles had a question. He looked at Kyle. "Will the project team be having team meetings?"

Kyle replied, "Of course." He looked at Sam. "Should we add those to the plan?"

Sam nodded. "That's a great idea. Yes, we should."

Kyle and the team took a few minutes to discuss what types of meetings made the most sense at this stage of the project, and they all agreed to take the Lean approach by planning daily huddle meetings.

Over the next thirty minutes, Kyle led the team as they discussed what and how they should communicate to the *high influence* stakeholders in order to maximize the stakeholders' engagement. Kyle contacted the stakeholders and confirmed their preferred medium of communication, and the dates and times for meetings. He also confirmed which team members should lead specific communications.

As they were working on in it, the Communication Plan looked like this.

Communication Plan

Audience	Message	Medium	Frequency	Timing	Responsibility
Emma Lewis	Update on schedule, performance, and value being delivered to customers and compare to the Business Case	In person in Emma's office	Monthly	First Monday at 3 p.m.	Kyle Jean-Francois
Eamon Lawlor	Updates on schedule, cost, scope control, waste, continuous improvements	In person meeting to present updates – located in obeya room	Every Monday morning	8:30 a.m.	Kyle
Max Lau	Internal and external resource use update	Conference call with a one-page update	Monthly	3rd Tuesday at 10 a.m.	Kyle
Juan Menez	Review of materials, spare parts list, and contracts	Phone call with copies of materials and spare parts plan	Every two weeks	Tuesday at 1 p.m.	Krisha

Audience	Message	Medium	Frequency	Timing	Responsibility
Kris King	Review of patent Searches and filings, review of formal contracts & agreements	Conference call with one-page update	Monthly	1st Monday at 1 p.m.	Kyle
Customers	Progress updates plus review of risks and issues	Visit in their offices	Quarterly	Fridays at 9 a.m., 10:30 a.m., 11 a.m.	Kyle Jean-Francois
All Stakeholders	Status updates on schedule & what to expect next	Meeting & video chat in obeya room with presentation	Monthly	1st Tuesday at 1 p.m.	Kyle
NBT Project Team	Daily prioritization and updates	Huddle meeting in obeya room	Daily	8:00am	Kyle

Kyle concluded by saying, "Going forward, I'll update this plan as often as needed. I'll display it here in our obeya room and on the obeya website so we can refer to it whenever we need to."

Adam leaned back in his chair and glanced over at Charles. "Charles, is there something you want to say about the Communication Plan?" The team erupted in laughter.

Charles set down his pen and looked up. "Why yes, Adam. This too was a helpful exercise. It's amazing how we can see all the important communications that need to take place, who the audience is, how and when it will be communicated, and who's assigned to deliver it – all on one page. Anyone could read it in less than a minute." Then the rest of the team chanted along with him. "That's Lean!"

Sam grinned. "At our next meeting we'll talk about Risk Management, and we'll also conduct a project risk assessment."

RISK MANAGEMENT

Kyle couldn't wait to learn how to properly conduct a risk assessment. He'd participated in assessments in the past, and had even tried to conduct them himself, but in every case the team members were too busy putting out "fires" to concentrate on proactively addressing risks. He wanted to uncover any and all project risks as soon as possible — before they snuck up on the team and became issues.

Sam welcomed everyone to the meeting. "Hello, team. There are three steps involved in managing risks: Identification, Assessment, and Response. We'll start by going through the first step, Risk Identification. Let's start by selecting some *categories* of risks, and then we'll list the risks that fall under those categories."

Step 1: Risk Identification

Kyle and the team decided to use the Work Breakdown Structure categories as the categories for risk identification, starting from left to right.

Sam gave each person a small pad of sticky notes and asked them to start with the first category and write each risk they could think of on a separate notepaper. "Do your best to describe the risk instead of just writing one word down." Some team members were already writing as she was talking, and some were already on their second and third sticky notes.

"This feels like therapy to me!" Kyle laughed as he spread his notes all around the table. He kept writing.

The others nodded in agreement as they filled up note after note with risks. Krisha was on her fifth risk already. "I've been burned so many times in the past. I'm not going to allow those things to happen again."

Charles was busy writing too. In all his years of practicing Lean, he had never participated in a risk assessment. "Do we have to stay within our own area of expertise, or can we list any risk we think could happen?"

"List any risks you can think of," Sam replied. "Also, keep in mind any and all risks that could impact the Triple Constraint – schedule, cost, and scope." The room was as quiet as a library while everyone was busy writing. They continued until they identified risks for each category in the work breakdown structure. Sam was writing too.

Step 2: Risk Assessment

When they finished writing down all the risks they could think of, Sam taped another poster to the wall. "I saw you writing a lot of risks down. You did a great job on Step One. The second step in practicing risk management is to assess the risks you just identified. Assessing them includes ranking them to show their potential level of impact. In other words, ask *how severe would they be?*

"Assessing also includes ranking them to show their level of probability. In other words, ask *how likely are they to occur?* Some assessments are quantitative and expressed in numbers, and some are qualitative and expressed in words. Our assessment will be qualitative."

Risks: Impact versus Probability of Occurrence

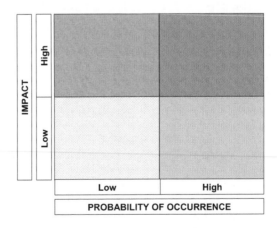

The poster showed four quadrants. A scale at the bottom showed low to high probability of occurrence, and a scale on the left side showed low to high impact to the project.

Sam asked each person to read out loud one of their risks from their stack of sticky notes, then she invited the group to discuss them, and asked them to decide which quadrant to place the sticky note in. Some people had written down virtually the same risks, so in those cases they only placed the risk on the poster once. The team went through each category until each person had stuck all their risks on the poster. In some cases, the team debated over which quadrant to place a risk in, but when they were finished, the poster showed risks in all four quadrants.

NBT Project Risks

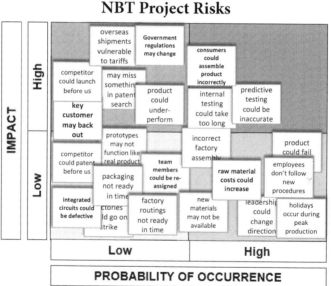

"There are so many risks! Maybe we should kill the project." Charles half joked.

Sam replied, "Well, we do have some concerns. But I don't see too many risks in the high impact and high probability boxes, so I don't think we need to kill the project – at least not yet."

She continued. "You all did a great job on the second step. Now I'll explain the final step. For each quadrant, there is an appropriate *risk response,* or action we should take." The she hung up a modified version of the same poster.

Risks and Responses

"If a risk has a low probability of occurring and a low impact on the project, you will document it but not take further action unless something changes. You will continue to monitor those risks throughout the life of the project to ensure they don't become more likely to occur or more severe."

Charles needed some clarification. "So, if it's in the low impact and low probability box we'll just keep it on our radar screen?"

"Exactly. Now, for the other boxes, if a risk has a high probability of occurrence and a low impact on the project, you'll create a contingency plan. The same applies if a risk has a high impact and low probability of occurrence."

She explained, "A *contingency plan* is a reactive risk response that is used *if* a specific risk turns into a reality. I like to think of a contingency plan as Plan B.

"Lastly, if a risk has a high probability and a high impact on the project, it is serious enough to require both a *mitigation plan* and a contingency plan. A mitigation plan is a proactive risk response strategy to reduce the probability of occurrence or impact of a risk."

"In other words, we'll need to get out the big guns for any risks in the high probability and high impact box!" Kyle suggested.

Sam nodded in agreement. "These risks are serious. We can't give them the chance to become issues – so we'll proactively plan to mitigate them.

"This part of the risk assessment will take some time, and fresh minds, so let's take a break and continue tomorrow. You've done a great job by identifying risks and determining how likely they are to happen, and what impact they would have. See you tomorrow for part three."

The next day, when the team arrived, they reviewed all the previous day's risks that were stuck to the poster. After getting some rest and clearing their minds, they had thought of a few more risks. They took a few minutes to go through the same steps, writing the risks on sticky notes and adding them to the poster, then ranking the probability that each risk would occur and its potential impact on the project.

Step 3: Risk Response

Sam continued with the next step. "Next, we'll move on to step three of risk management: risk response."

"Risk response involves determining a strategy for the risks identified. In other words, what will the team do to address and reduce the impact and probability of each risk? It's more challenging to get through this step, especially on large or complex project with many risks — like this one."

Kyle agreed. This is where the work on his previous risk assessments had stopped. The team members didn't know how to move forward with addressing the risks, and they didn't want to take the time to think them through.

Sam continued, "Once the risks have been identified, assessed, and assigned corresponding mitigation and/or contingency plans, they should be logged in a project risk register. The register can be a spreadsheet or something similar that works for the team." Then she showed the team a basic example of what a risk register looks like.

Risk Register

Risk	Probability	Impact	Mitigation	Contingency	Owner

Kyle led the team as they started with the high probability-high impact risks. They transferred the sticky notes from the Impact versus Probability poster to the Risk Register poster, and then they discussed what the corresponding mitigation plan should be for each risk. Once they agreed, Kyle documented it on the poster.

Then they discussed what the corresponding contingency plans should be. Some of the responses included applying Lean tools and techniques. Lastly, they determined an "owner," the most appropriate person to oversee each risk response.

As they were working on it, the Risk Register looked like this.

NBT Risk Register

Risk	Proba-bility	Impact	Mitigation	Contingency	Owner
Consumers could assemble product incorrectly	High	High	Practice poka-yoke, design, pretest with 'test' consumers	Modify instruction sheets	Kyle
Predictive testing could be inaccurate	High	High	Confirm the latest version of predictive software is installed and used	Test with prototypes and engineering samples to conduct physical testing during pilot phases	Krisha

Risk	Probability	Impact	Mitigation	Contingency	Owner
Internal testing could take too long	High	High	Certify external back-up sources for testing	Add time to the schedule to allow for all testing to be completed, and alert stakeholders	Krisha
Government regulations may change	Low	High	–	Add time to the schedule to address and alert stakeholders	Kyle

When they finished, the poster showed risk responses for everything except the low impact-low probability risks. Those would remain on a "watch list."

"You've done a lot of important work today," Sam told them.

The next day, the team revisited the *Current versus Desired State* portion of their stakeholder assessment. Since some of the stakeholders were not at the *desired* state of engagement, this was a risk *to* the project. The team worked together to develop and document mitigation approaches that would encourage those stakeholders to be more engaged.

Some of the mitigations included organizational change management plans, including: raising awareness, showing each stakeholder the WIIFM's *(what's in it for me?)*, updating the communication plan by adding more frequent one-on-one communications, providing training, and more.

When they were finished with the risk assessment, Charles offered his feedback. "In all seriousness, this was a helpful exercise. It frightens me to see all the risks associated with this project, but it would frighten me *more* if we had not gone through the exercise of identifying them all. Now we can see all our high-level risks as well as our action plans – all on one page. It might take slightly more than a minute to read because there are many risks, but it's definitely Lean!"

Sam replied. "Thank you for your input, Charles."

Kyle was thrilled to see Charles participating in the creation of risk mitigation and contingency plans. He thought to himself, *maybe this knowledge will reduce the odds of him dropping stink bombs (risks and issues) on us and then running away, leaving us to try to solve them ourselves.* He commented, "I'll hang the Risk Register here in the obeya room and also post it on our obeya website."

"That sounds great, Kyle," Sam responded. "There are two important things to keep in mind as you manage risks:

1. You will need to build the mitigations into your project plan because they'll probably incur some costs, require some resources and take some time.
2. You will also want to also share your highest-level risks with your project sponsor, Eamon. Let him know your mitigation and contingency plans and get any additional input or suggestions he may have."

Kyle agreed. He was relieved to have the risk assessment completed properly this time, and he thought the mitigation and contingency plans were realistic. He added, "As we approach our next major milestone, I can arrange time for the team to re-visit the risk assessment to see if anything needs to be removed or added."

"Perfect!" Sam replied. "Next, we'll continue the Planning Phase of our project by creating a Procurement Plan."

PROCUREMENT PLAN

Early the following week, Sam and Kyle met with the procurement stakeholders who would be the project go-to sources for all things related to procurements. Some of them had participated in the creation of the work breakdown structure, and now they would provide more information for the Procurement Plan.

Kyle reviewed the procurement work that would be needed for the project. His list included things like:

- The hiring of and contracts for temporary workers.
- The purchasing of various materials and items for development, prototyping and testing purposes.

- Statements of Work (SOWs) for items manufactured or work completed by outside companies.
- Software agreements, licenses and renewals.
- Confidentiality agreements for temporary product testers outside the company.
- Any other agreements for work to be completed outside The Flying Machine.

The team wasn't sure yet if some component parts should be manufactured by The Flying Machine or if it would make more sense to outsource them. In those cases, the team would need to go through a make-buy decision process. So, Kyle shared which make-buy decisions still needed to be made by the team, and by what date. They discussed how the make-buy analyses could be calculated.

Together they documented what needed to be procured, what would be needed for requests for proposals (RFPs), or requests for quotations (RFQs), sourcing contracts, statements of work, and purchase orders. They documented the supplier selection criteria, and the supplier deadlines needed to keep the project on track and to meet cost targets.

They documented which member of The Flying Machine would be the go-to person in contact with the suppliers, who would monitor the supplier's progress, the supplier's quality and final deliveries, and which member of The Flying Machine would ultimately close the contracts. They decided to meet every week for a procurement update, so Kyle added that meeting to the Communication Plan.

The next day, Kyle, the procurement stakeholders, and the project team met to review the Procurement Plan and provide input.

The project team was concerned that the process of generating purchase orders required excessive layers of approvals and would waste valuable time. In some cases, it took longer to generate a purchase order than it did to complete the work funded by the PO. So, the procurement stakeholders agreed that over the next few weeks they would conduct a current state and future state value stream mapping exercise of the process to generate a purchase order. They planned to identify areas of needed improvement and potential kaizen events to "Lean out" the PO request process.

Everyone seemed satisfied with the go-forward plan, especially Kyle.

QUALITY PLAN

At the next team meeting, Sam discussed the Quality Plan. She explained to the team, "On a poorly planned project, team members and stakeholders will debate mid-way through the project as to what quality is and what minimum quality is acceptable for project sign-off. Instead, quality should be defined during the Planning Phase so there is no debate later as to what quality we need for different aspects of the project."

Over the next hour, Kyle led the team as they worked chronologically through each step of the product development process and documented the types of quality metrics that they needed to track and assess the work throughout the project. The team reached agreement on what quality levels would be considered acceptable for the project to move on to the next lifecycle phase and finally to completion. Here are some examples of the quality metrics they adopted.

NBT Product Related Metrics

1. Product form and function (the maximum allowable quantity of units that do not meet specifications).
2. Decibel levels (the maximum allowable quantity of units that exceed noise levels)
3. RFI levels (the maximum allowable quantity of units that exceed radio frequency interference levels).
4. Supplier quality (maximum allowable quantity of defective components coming from suppliers).
5. Battery life (maximum allowable quantity of units that fall short of the expected battery life).
6. Maximum quantity of engineering pilots/iterations completed before final approval for production.
7. Minimum quantity of assembly workers to be trained to assemble and package the product.
8. Minimum quantity of test units to be pre-tested by future users during product development.
9. Projected sales versus actual orders.
10. Consumer satisfaction (maximum allowable quantity of calls/online complaints/service center visits)

NBT Project Related Metrics

1. Minimum number of Gemba walks in each key area — to further understand how things are done today and to get input from the people who are *doing* the work.
2. Target lines of code completed per week by programmers.
3. Schedule and cost targets for each major milestone (design reviews, mold release).
4. Minimum number of quotes received from separate sources

for all things purchased.

5. Minimum quantity of backup sources in case of a shortage of purchased supplies.

It was tempting to add additional items to measure, but the team was careful to measure only what was important for the success of the project and what the customer valued. Measuring anything else would be considered wasteful, and not Lean.

They also discussed several ways to build poka-yoke (error-proofing) steps into the product and their processes to reduce or eliminate the odds of mistakes happening.

Sam wrapped up the meeting. "Great input, everyone. Next, we'll conquer our last task for the Planning Phase – our Scope Change Management Plan."

SCOPE CHANGE MANAGEMENT PLAN

At the next team gathering, Sam addressed the group. "When you created the NBT Project Charter, you put significant effort into defining the scope of the project. Going forward, you'll need to manage it well. You'll need to make sure the only work being done is what was committed to in the Charter, what the customer demands or pulls, and what the customer values. You shouldn't work on deviations from that without going through a change control process. Otherwise you'll mess up the flow of your work."

Charles couldn't hold in his opinion. "I vote we just tell people no! There are no scope changes allowed!"

"I wish it was that easy." Sam explained, "Sometimes it can be tricky to detect a scope change when it's happening, and sometimes scope changes are necessary. For example, if a competitor introduces a similar product with a new feature that consumers love and begin to expect, we cannot introduce our new product without it or something better. Sometimes changes are necessary."

Kyle paraphrased. "So, not all scope changes are bad – they are just not part of the original plan."

"That's right, Kyle," Sam replied. "Your job is to recognize a potential scope change when you see one. Also, if someone requests a scope change, you'll need to document the request, assess the impact on cost, schedule, performance, level of risk, etcetera, approve or reject the request, and either make the change or let the requestor know why the change wasn't made. So, you'll need to determine who has the authority to approve or reject the change requests."

Charles thought for a second and then spoke up. "I'd like to believe that this process already exists and that we don't have to create one from scratch."

Kyle responded, "If we *had* an existing process, and we *followed* it, we wouldn't be so messed up today. Our projects are never on time because we're constantly making uncontrolled changes that don't require any approvals."

"No worries." Sam jumped in. "We can quickly create a change control process that should work, as long as everyone is willing to follow it. Once it's created, Kyle, you should get Eamon's input and his approval since he's the project sponsor. Once you have that, you should explain the scope change process to all the stakeholders, so they know it's a formal process to be followed."

The team spent the next fifteen minutes creating the process.

NBT Scope Change Process

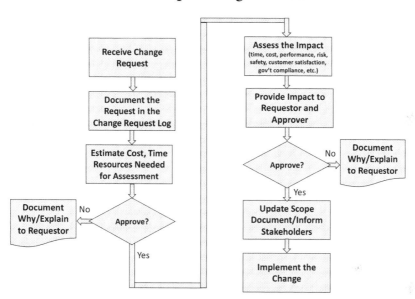

Later, Adam created a simple online Change Request Form and a Scope Change Log.

Scope Change Log

Requestor	Date	Description	Impact of Rejecting the Change	Alternative Option	Status

Kyle stored the log in the shared team obeya site. He also reviewed the process with Eamon, who approved it. Eamon agreed that as the project sponsor, he would be responsible to approve or deny scope change requests. If he was not available for a review and approval within twenty-four hours, Sam would be the approver, so there would be no bottlenecks for approvals.

At the first monthly stakeholder meeting, Kyle shared the Scope Change Process, the Change Request Form, and the Scope Change Log.

There were some other templates the team needed, like an action log, an issues log, and a decision log. Kyle had looked around to see if there were any existing templates already being used on other projects. He was pleasantly surprised to find them. He explained to the team, "These existing templates are considered to be standard work. We can use them, so we don't need to create unnecessary work, otherwise known as waste." Adam added the logs to the obeya room and on the obeya website for all the stakeholders to see and for the team to contribute to at any time.

It took the team a while to complete all the plans in the Planning Phase, but they all felt it was time well spent.

Krisha felt confident. "I think this project has a strong foundation. It would take a catastrophic event to get us off course."

Sam was glad to hear her feedback. "Thank you to everyone on the team for your input during the Planning Phase. This should help you work efficiently going forward. Let's wrap up the Planning Phase tomorrow by documenting the lessons learned."

DOCUMENTING LESSONS LEARNED

The next morning, Kyle thought about the lessons he had learned throughout the Planning Phase. Later, he met with the team to discuss and document everyone's lessons learned.

HOW TO MAKE IT LEAN

After the team finished documenting all the lessons they had learned during the Planning Phase, they talked about the benefits of adding Lean principles.

Krisha was first to add her thoughts. "A picture is worth a thousand words. That said, our obeya room and obeya site, along with the visual displays we're providing, are really helping our stakeholders understand every aspect of our project."

Kyle agreed and added his opinion. "In the past, when we were giving status updates, you could tell by the look on some people's faces that they just didn't understand what we were explaining."

Jean-Francois had to jump in. "On another topic, I can already tell a difference in the way our team operates now that we're applying 5S to our work areas and electronic files. I'm more organized, and I can quickly find the information I'm looking for. My time is spent on more productive tasks these days, and I like it!"

When they finished their discussion, they worked together to create a table showing the project management activities needed for the Planning Phase and the corresponding Lean activities.

How to Make the Planning Phase Lean

Project Management Activity	How to Make It Lean
Finalize the Project Management Plan.	Use standard work whenever possible (templates, processes, etc.)
Schedule management: create a Work Breakdown Structure, estimate the project schedule, document key milestones, and determine the critical path.	Add planned kaizen and kaikaku events to the Work Breakdown Structure and to the project schedule.

Project Management Activity	How to Make It Lean
Assemble the initial project team.	Practice obeya by securing a project "war room" for visual displays and metrics. Practice the "T" in DOWNTIME to reduce transportation waste by co-locating the team and minimizing travel between team members. Encourage the team to practice 5S with workspaces and electronic document storage. Provide Lean training for the team.
Resource management — determine team member roles and responsibilities.	Beware of the "W" and "N" in DOWNTIME, such as waiting for work to begin and non-utilizing or under-leveraging subject matter experts. Add both project management and Lean deliverables to team members' performance evaluations. Practice Just in Time (JIT), ensuring no team members are waiting for work to be assigned or causing bottlenecks due to being overloaded.

Project Management Activity	How to Make It Lean
Apply the Cost Management Plan.	Be on the lookout for muda, muri, mura, and the eight forms of waste.
Apply the Stakeholder Management Plan.	Periodically invite stakeholders to huddles, kaizen, and kaikaku events.
Apply the Communication Management Plan.	Conduct daily huddles to keep team members on track. Use visual management boards to simplify or summarize information and to help stakeholders understand complex topics. Invite stakeholders to the obeya room to see the value stream maps and visual displays.
Apply the Risk Management plan.	Post the Risk Assessments and Risk Responses in the obeya room so they remain transparent and "living" documents.
Apply the Procurement Management Plan.	Eliminate waste and enable flow by generating efficient approval processes and contracts that don't require excessive layers of approvals.

Project Management Activity	How to Make It Lean
Apply the Quality Management Plan.	Continually look for ways to improve processes. Build poka-yoke into projects and products to reduce the odds of mistakes happening.
Apply the Scope Management Plan.	Ensure the only work being done is what the customer demands or considers to be of value.

Executing a Project

Once the project was officially in the Execution Phase, Kyle led the team as they worked according to their Project Management Plan. In parallel, they continued to follow The Flying Machine's existing Product Development Process.

PERFORMING WORK ACCORDING TO THE PLAN

Needless to say, the team had several working meetings. At first, Charles complained. "I can't get my work done because I'm in meetings all the time."

But Kyle pushed back. "Charles, we're discussing important topics, making decisions, and solving problems in our meetings. This is how we're getting most of our work done. If *we* aren't taking care of these things, who would be?"

Charles backed down. "I guess you're right." He only wanted the chance to express his opinion. After that, during future meetings he transitioned from feeling like a victim to feeling like a guy who *gets things done.*

But Kyle took to heart what Charles said, and he made every effort to hold the most productive meetings possible. He did his best to be prepared before each meeting. He sent out agendas in advance. He only invited the people who absolutely needed to be there. If decisions or a consensus was needed, he practiced nemawashi, meeting with people in advance to go over a specific topic and getting their input and buy-in prior to the more formal meeting.

During each meeting he appointed a note-taker to record the meeting minutes. They documented the action items, who was assigned to each action and the targeted completion date. During each meeting, the team actively discussed actions, issues, and risks. Kyle encouraged everyone to participate. When the meetings ended, there were no questions as to what direction the team was headed in and what action items needed to be addressed.

After each meeting Kyle was diligent, and sent out the meeting minutes to each person who attended (or missed) the meetings – complete with a summarized list of action items, issues and risks.

Also, he did his best to ensure that the project flowed without interruptions. The team used existing standard work wherever possible, and where opportunities existed, they made continuous improvements. If new work was being created, they did their best to make it repeatable standard work.

They took time to identify all existing processes that were relevant to the NBT project. If an existing value stream map didn't exist, they created one. They documented steps in each process that worked well and highlighted kaizen opportunities for areas that didn't work well. By the time they were finished they had future state value stream maps for all the relevant processes. They posted the new maps in the obeya room and on the obeya website.

Finally, they completed the final design of the NBT product. They conducted computer model simulation testing. They built prototypes, conducted lab testing, designed and built molds and dies, ordered manufacturing and assembly equipment, designed the packaging, and built pre-production samples on the assembly line.

STAKEHOLDER MANAGEMENT

While they were executing the project, Kyle had dozens of stakeholders to manage. At times it was excruciatingly difficult. Some were easy to please and to keep updated, while others were difficult to find and to keep updated. One or two were constantly questioning whether the NBT project was the right product or not, or whether the product had the right features or not. Some thought the team should be using different technology for engineering and programming and prototyping. Kyle had to keep in constant contact with them all and make sure their questions were being addressed. At times it was exhausting, but he made it a priority.

He made a point of inviting stakeholders to kaizen and kaikaku events so they could get a close-up view of the challenges the team had to overcome. He also invited stakeholders to occasional team huddle meetings so they could see the team in action as they prioritized their work and tackled the day-to-day challenges.

To share knowledge and to optimize communication and transparency, Kyle held all stakeholder meetings in the obeya room. He also encouraged stakeholders to frequently visit the obeya room and the obeya website in-between the stakeholder meetings so they could see the most up-to-date value stream maps, visual displays, metrics and more.

TEAM BUILDING AND CONFLICT RESOLUTION

Team building occurred naturally as the team members worked closely together to complete their work within the Planning Phase. For example, the collaborative creation of the various documents — the charter, stakeholder assessment, WBS, RACI chart, risk assessment and the communication plan enabled the team members to get to know each other, and to build accountability and trust. The team continued to bond as its members worked together to conduct kaizen and kaikaku events, create A3s, and solve problems.

Kyle was lucky to inherit a team of people who were skilled and got along well with each other — for the most part. Occasionally, personality clashes occurred. Krisha was impatient sometimes and seemed condescending to some people. Adam was sarcastic with people who were less tech-savvy. Charles was over-the-top loud and demanding most of the time. Jean-Francois traveled most of the time and missed lots of meetings. Regardless, Kyle was able to manage the team.

Throughout the Execution Phase, Sam spent less and less time with the NBT team as Kyle's skills and confidence increased.

But one afternoon, while Sam was in her office, Krisha popped in. "Heads-up. A big scene just went down in the factory, and it was about the NBT project!" Krisha said.

As Krisha was backing out the door, Kyle was rushing in. His cheeks were red with frustration. "Sam, I just can't take it anymore! Charles is being a major jerk face!"

He walked over to an empty chair and sat down. Shaking his head and staring at the floor, he mumbled under his breath. "He's a freakin' nut case!"

Sam immediately stopped what she was doing. She closed her laptop and put her mobile phone in a drawer. She gave Kyle her full attention and complete eye contact.

"Why is Charles is being a ..." She stopped and re-thought her question. "What happened that upset you?"

Kyle took a few seconds to calm down, and then he quickly explained the issue to her.

"The controller unit pilot manufacturing run is falling behind. This could jeopardize the entire project schedule. So, on the pilot production line, I rearranged some of the process steps and cut out some steps in order to get the units produced faster." He paused. "Then Charles showed up and accused me of violating the *now in place* future state process! He ranted on about how the team carefully mapped out the current state process, completed kaizen events, and agreed on the new process — *as if I don't know that.* He said I 'came out of nowhere and screwed up the flow,' allowing waste to reenter the process. He said I was gonna ruin the NBT project and let Tornado beat us to the market. When I tried to explain why I did what I did, he called me an 'anti-Lean cowboy.' Then he told me to 'go rogue on my own time' and to 'get lost.' You know he chased me out of the factory?"

Sam took a deep breath and thought about how to handle the situation. It needed to be addressed, and now. The NBT project was too important to be dragged down or delayed due to a team conflict.

Over the next fifteen minutes, she listened carefully as Kyle again explained what had happened. A couple of times she was tempted to jump in and start fixing the situation, but instead she let Kyle finish.

She thought it was important to develop her team members, especially those who were emerging leaders. That meant encouraging them to fight their own battles and to solve their own problems. She thought about how practicing Lean meant creating a culture of empowerment.

So, after Kyle had completely calmed down, she began coaching him on how to solve the problem himself. She explained to him that a project manager needs to be a good leader and a role model for others to follow. She reminded him that practicing Lean involves being empowered. She explained how the word "flow" means eliminating opportunities for manufacturing waste, and it also means eliminating wasted team member efforts. If team members have unhealthy conflicts, the project does not flow. "It's the project manager's job to manage team conflicts to ensure the project flows," she explained.

She encouraged him to talk face-to-face with Charles and to work with him on a resolution. After some convincing, Kyle agreed.

They role-played a little so he could practice saying a few constructive things to Charles. "If that doesn't work, come back, and I'll step in to help," she promised.

Kyle seemed relieved and up to the task. As he stood up to leave, Sam had one more request. "Oh, and please don't wait until you can't take it anymore! If you're seeing a problem you can't resolve quickly, escalate it, and let's tackle it right away."

She also gently reminded him, "I'm always here to listen and help, but don't forget that Eamon is the project sponsor for this project. You should feel comfortable escalating problems to him." Kyle replied by giving two thumbs up.

The next morning, Sam was relieved to learn that Kyle and Charles had worked through the conflict and reestablished their working relationship. Kyle realized that he had made a mistake by potentially reversing the future state process that the team worked hard to create. Charles realized that his conversation with Kyle should have been handled much more professionally. Then the two of them worked together on a plan that would get the controller unit pilot back on schedule.

MANAGING CONTRACTS

Throughout the Execution Phase, the team managed various contracts and suppliers. While purchasing components needed for pre-production samples, they were careful to watch for waste and avoided building excess inventory. They planned for Just in Time (JIT) delivery of production components. They even invited their suppliers to participate in kaizen and kaikaku events.

TRACKING AND ADDRESSING ISSUES

Kyle continued hosting daily huddle meetings that included the primary team members. He reserved time during the huddles to discuss and log issues. When an issue was raised, the team took extra time to be sure they understood the root cause of the issue. Thinking through the "A" in the DMAIC process, they analyzed root causes, process inputs, and outputs. Sometimes they asked the Five Whys, and sometimes they used the A3 process to document problems and get to their root causes.

EXECUTING RISK CONTINGENCIES

As the project progressed, the team continued to monitor the risks. Kyle always reserved time during team huddle meetings to discuss any new risks. It was interesting to see which risks turned into issues and which ones didn't.

They were able to remove some risks from their Risk Log, as the likelihood of them happening had gone away completely. But they also needed to add a few risks based on some newer circumstances that didn't exist when the team originally created their risk assessment.

In some cases, they needed to deploy their risk contingency plans. In those cases, they reassessed the triple constraint to see if there was any impact to the project cost, scope or schedule. If there was, they took swift corrective actions. Any delays in the schedule would jeopardize The Flying Machine's ability to beat Tornado to the market. Any increases in cost would reduce The Flying Machine's profits and possibly the value to the customer.

MAKING PROCESS IMPROVEMENTS

The team continued to identify existing processes that needed to be improved. They developed a culture of continuous improvement by creating current state process maps, highlighting areas for improvement, and then holding kaizen or kaikaku events to address them.

For example, The Flying Machine liked to provide customers with prototypes (working models) of new products, as it greatly increased the odds of customers buying the coming new products. But the current process of creating prototypes was too slow. If The Flying Machine couldn't supply working protypes quickly enough, customers could get their prototypes from The Flying Machine's competitor, Tornado, instead. So, with input from subject matter experts, the team mapped out the current state process of ordering a new prototype machine and creating prototypes for customers.

Current State Process: Creating Prototypes

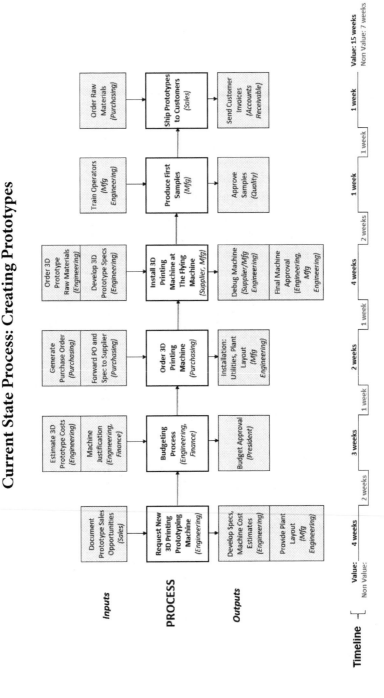

The team documented each step in the process along with the inputs to and outputs from each step. They also documented the time it took to complete the value added and non-value-added steps. When they were finished, they discussed where problem areas existed. They highlighted each identified problem as a kaizen opportunity and drew a starburst around it.

Current State Process: Creating Prototypes
(with kaizen opportunities)

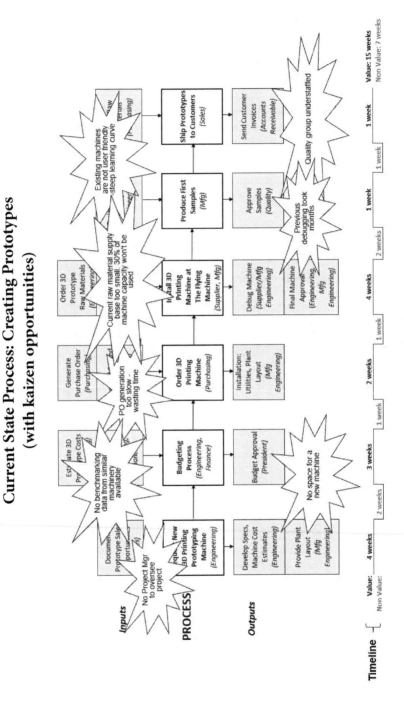

Once the current state map was completed, they created a future state process map. To eliminate the highlighted problems from the current state, they scheduled and planned kaizen events.

When the team was finished, they had a new process that enabled them to deliver prototypes to customers much faster than before. According to feedback they received from their customers, The Flying Machine's new prototype delivery time was much faster than their competitor Tornado's delivery time. The new process worked well.

"Let's not keep this a secret." Sam reminded the team that there were other divisions within The Flying Machine that had inefficient processes for ordering new machines and creating prototypes. The team worked together on a plan to apply yokoten (rapid sharing across the organization). They did this by sharing their newly successful process so it could be used in other areas across the company within a short timeframe.

TRACKING PROGRESS

Kyle tracked the project's progress against the original baselines. He reported metrics and gave regular status updates to the team and the stakeholders. He focused on reporting only the information that the stakeholders wanted and needed and was careful not to overproduce.

To share complex technical information in ways that were easy to read and understand, Kyle continued to apply what he had learned during the Lean training sessions about visual management, visual management boards, and visual control methods. He took every opportunity to show simple pictures and charts, which quickly and easily got the messages across to the key stakeholders. He also displayed up-to-date visual information in the obeya room and on the obeya site.

In project status meetings with Eamon and Emma, Kyle provided updates on the project's schedule, cost, and product performance compared to the value the customers were expecting.

When issues came up that caused an unexpected cost increase or a schedule delay, Kyle was honest. As much as he wanted to tell them everything was perfect, there were times when he had to report problems. In those cases, he made sure the team took the time they needed to investigate and understand the root causes of the problems. He made sure they had a plan to get back on track. The project's true status as well as the plan to get back on track was reported at the same time.

Eamon and Emma were relieved to know that Kyle was aware of the problems, the root causes of the problems, and that he and the team had plans to address them. They were amazed, so far at least, at the lack of firefighting that had taken place. They were accustomed to seeing much more turmoil and project stress by this point in the company's projects.

DOCUMENTING LESSONS LEARNED

The next morning, Kyle thought about the lessons he had learned throughout the Execution Phase. Later, he met with the team to discuss and document everyone's lessons learned.

HOW TO MAKE IT LEAN

After the team finished documenting all the lessons they had learned during the Execution Phase, they talked about the benefits of adding Lean principles.

Eamon commented first. "It really helps that when we provide project status updates, we also give an update on the value we're delivering to the customer. In the past we didn't do that, and we lost sight along the way of what the customer expected. Now we're on track to deliver what the customer expects because we're thinking about it all the time."

Then Adam added his thoughts. "I've been creating A3s to understand the root cause of problems, and to prioritize potential countermeasures. I also catch myself asking the Five Whys, or even more. Solving a problem is so much easier when you take time to understand what caused it in the first place."

When they finished their discussion, the team worked together to create a table showing the project management activities needed for the Executing Phase and the corresponding Lean activities.

How to Make the Execution Phase Lean

Project Management Activity	How to Make It Lean
Perform work according to the plan.	Manage the project to flow without interruptions. Create and use repeatable, standard work.
Manage stakeholders.	Keep stakeholders engaged with consistent communication, inviting them to the obeya room, providing transparency with visual displays and metrics.
Practice team building and conflict resolution. Evaluate team performance and resolve any conflicts.	Encourage team participation in the creation of A3s, the Work Breakdown Structure, Risk Assessment, Communication Plan, kaizen and kaikaku events to accomplish goals while building team relationships, accountability, and trust.
Manage contracts, select suppliers and manage suppliers.	When purchasing goods, beware of waste with excess inventory and practice Just in Time delivery. Invite awarded suppliers to participate in kaizen and kaikaku events.

Project Management Activity	How to Make It Lean
Document, track and address issues.	Reserve time during team huddles to discuss and log issues.
Execute risk contingency plans.	Follow standard work during the risk assessment process. Reserve time to update risks during huddle meetings.
Make process improvements.	Follow-up on actions arising from kaizen events and kaikaku events. Apply yokoten to quickly share learnings and improvements across the organization.
Track progress and report to sponsor and stakeholders.	Use visual management, visual management boards, and visual control to show the project status and metrics. Apply the "I" in DMAIC: Improve by reducing defects and improving current processes. Show progress compared to the value the customer is expecting.

Monitoring and Controlling a Project

The entire time the team was executing the project, Kyle took steps to monitor and control the project.

MEASURING PERFORMANCE

He constantly measured the project against the original baselines that were set up during the Planning Phase. As the product was being developed, Kyle regularly checked to make sure its performance was aligned with the "Voice of the Customer" expectations.

MEETING INTERMEDIATE MILESTONES

As the team worked to meet the intermediate milestones, Kyle checked to make sure they were also meeting the objectives of the future state value stream maps. He applied corrective actions when necessary to keep the project on track.

CONTROLLING SCOPE

Several changes were requested, even more than Kyle had expected. He and the team had thought that the Project Charter was clear about what *was and was not* in scope, but it was hard to determine whether some requests were in scope or not.

Some were obvious scope changes, like the request for an increased packaging size and the request for a better version of the controller software.

Other change requests were more subtle, and it was difficult to tell if they were actual scope changes or not. For example, the team spent some time trying to decide if a customer's request to modify the frequency of the drone's flashing lights was a scope change or not. They determined the impact of making the change and decided it was not a scope change, but more of a refined specification. There were lots of instances when the team had to take time away from their daily work to assess whether a not a request was a scope change or not, and how the project would be impacted by making the change.

They documented all the scope change requests in the Scope Change Log. It was critical to have all the changes recorded in the Log because there were some cases when a change was requested and the team had spent a significant amount of time assessing the impact. The change was denied, but then a month or two later someone else requested a similar change. Since the team had the original request logged and they noted that it had been denied, along with the reason why, they didn't need to waste time doing another assessment of the impact only to deny it again.

Being Lean includes managing scope changes efficiently, so Kyle made sure the process flowed, and that it didn't take excessive amounts of time to assess the impacts of potential changes. He checked often to make sure the team was only focused on what the customer required, requested, and would consider to be of value.

MONITORING REVISED PROCESSES

The team created several new processes with corresponding value stream maps. They also revised some of the existing processes. During the Monitoring and Controlling Phase they checked the new and revised processes to make sure they provided the expected customer value. They also monitored the processes for further continuous improvement opportunities.

MONITORING STAKEHOLDER ENGAGEMENT

During the Planning Phase the team analyzed each key stakeholder's level of engagement. They documented the current state of the stakeholder's engagement as well as the level of engagement needed for the project's success.

In the Monitoring and Controlling Phase, Kyle worked to keep the stakeholders engaged by continuously communicating with them. He encouraged them to visit the obeya room and the obeya website, and to read the project status documents and the graphic metric reports. He also invited them to participate in continuous improvement tasks.

DOCUMENTING LESSONS LEARNED

Kyle led the team as they documented the lessons they learned while monitoring and controlling the project.

HOW TO MAKE IT LEAN

After the team finished documenting all the lessons they had learned, they talked about the benefits of adding Lean principles.

Krisha was first to add her input. "This project flows. I don't see the major bottlenecks our past projects have had. Changes are assessed, reviewed, and approved efficiently."

And then Charles jumped in. "I really appreciate how the whole team is thinking about continuous improvement. In the past, there were only a couple of people in the entire company focused on CI. Now it's everyone's job, and it's part of our culture."

Kyle nodded in agreement. "I'm grateful for the extra time we took at the beginning of the project to carefully measure and set baselines in several areas. In the past we reported that we were making progress, but we had nothing to compare the progress to. Now we can provide credible reports that illustrate where we are today versus the original baselines."

When they finished their discussion, they worked together to create a table showing the project management activities needed while monitoring and controlling a project, along with the corresponding Lean activities.

How to Make the Monitoring and Controlling Phase Lean

Project Management Activity	How to Make It Lean
Measure performance against baseline. Apply corrective actions to variances.	Apply quality control. Revisit baselines set in the DMAIC "Define" stage. Check for the "D" in DOWNTIME (defects). Ensure to-date performance is still aligned with the Voice of the Customer.
Meet intermediate milestones.	Apply the "M" from DMAIC by measuring intermediate milestones.
Control scope by assessing, approving/denying, and managing scope changes.	Revisit the Eight Forms of Waste to ensure that the team is not over-producing and excessive time is not spent waiting for decisions on scope changes. Compare against DMAIC "control" documentation.
Monitor new and revised processes to confirm they are correct and effective.	Meet the objectives of the Future State Value Stream Map.

Closing a Project

CONFIRMING THE WORK IS COMPLETED

The team was excited when the first pre-production products were made in the factory. After they confirmed that the manufacturing and assembly processes met their expectations, they made fifty production quality units. Charles led the team through a quality check and a final review for defects. It took a couple of weeks, but eventually every new product component, every new piece of machinery, and every manufacturing process step passed all the internal and independent third-party inspections.

OBTAINING FORMAL ACCEPTANCE

The next step was to obtain formal acceptance by the sponsor. Kyle first conducted an informal nemawashi meeting with Eamon to gain his acceptance. Then the project was formally accepted by Eamon, who advised his boss, the CEO, Emma. Once again, they were amazed at the lack of firefighting, stress, and turmoil that had taken place on the project.

By this time there were three large external customers, and their acceptance was required too. The customers had earlier agreed to the upfront deliverables, and Kyle had been giving them regular status updates. Now that that project was completed, he provided formal documentation including certifications and quality inspection results. Then he and Jean-Francois met with each customer in person to get their acceptance and feedback.

All three customers formally accepted the project as being completed. In fact, they placed orders and wanted their shipments delivered as soon as possible!

HANDING OFF THE FINAL PROJECT

A product like this one required continued attention after the production launch. After-market parts and services needed to be available for many years to follow.

An after-market service support team was assigned to take on the post-production stage of the project. Kyle and his team set up a series of transition and knowledge transfer sessions held in the obeya room. They shared all the project- and product related information with the support team. Together they mapped out a plan for continuous support, continuous improvement, and alignment with the customers' expectations.

CLOSING CONTRACTS

When Kyle let the team know that Eamon and the three customers had formally accepted the project, all the project team members cheered.

Charles was the most animated. "Happy hour! Let's go!"

"That sounds like a great idea," Kyle responded. "But we have a few more things to wrap up first." The team moved efficiently and wasted no time as they closed all the project documents including the contracts and purchase orders.

RELEASING RESOURCES

Kyle met with the team members' managers to let them know the project was coming to an end, and that their staff members would soon be available to work on other projects.

REPORTING FINAL PROGRESS STATUS

Kyle and the team compared the NBT project's completion time to that of similar past projects. The early phases of the NBT project took a little longer than in previous projects, but the execution and closing phases took significantly less time. Overall, there was about a twenty percent reduction in the project schedule.

Kyle prepared two final status reports. One was for customers, and the other was for internal stakeholders including Eamon and Emma.

The report for customers showed that the project and product met all the deliverables, including the design, performance, quality, and safety expectations. It also showed when the customer would receive their first shipment and a plan for customer support going forward.

The report for the internal stakeholders showed the above items plus the final cost and completion date in comparison to the original baseline. It showed that the Future State Value Stream Maps were in place and had become the new Current State maps. The report also showed the twenty percent schedule reduction. At the end, it showed the plan for continuous improvement and the plan for product support going forward.

As part of the internal report, Jean-Francois shared the Business Case, comparing the original baseline goals to the new current state. Because the project met its cost and delivery targets, The Flying Machine was in a good position to manufacture the product at the expected sales volume levels and to reach the expected profitability.

This was excellent news, because the profit goals for this new high-tech product were the highest of all the new products at The Flying Machine. In fact, it was the best news Emma had heard since she joined the company.

DOCUMENTING FINAL LESSONS LEARNED

Kyle led the team as they documented the lessons they had learned throughout the Closing Phase.

HOW TO MAKE IT LEAN

After the team finished documenting all the lessons they learned, they talked about the benefits of adding Lean principles.

Kyle spoke first. "I'm amazed that we created *future state* value stream maps that are now our *current state* maps! It proves that if you have a vision and a plan, you can make it a reality." The rest of the team smiled and nodded in agreement.

"I guess that's what Sam meant what she talked about empowerment," Adam added. "We were empowered to make things happen, and we did!"

"Now we need to make the changes stick and not revert back to our old ways," Charles replied as he gave a quick glance toward Kyle.

Kyle met the implied challenge with a grin. "We'll do even better than that. We'll sustain the new processes we created. And as we learn more about how they're working for us, we'll continuously improve them."

When they finished their discussion, they worked together to create a table showing the project management activities needed while closing a project, along with the corresponding Lean activities.

How to Make the Closing Phase Lean

Project Management Activity	How to Make It Lean
Confirm work is completed.	Conduct a quality check and a final review for defects. Apply the "C" in DMAIC to control by embedding changes, tracking improvements and ensuring sustainability.
Obtain formal acceptance from the sponsor and customers, and document their feedback.	Conduct nemawashi to gain approval on the deliverables before holding formal sign-off meetings.
Hand-off the final project and transfer knowledge for continuous improvement by a support team.	Develop a plan for continuous improvement and continued alignment with customer expectations.
Close contracts, budgets, and purchase orders.	Move efficiently to avoid waste such as excess processing time taken to close formal documents and processes.
Release resources.	Avoid waste, such as having non-utilized talent attending meetings or receiving emails.

Project Management Activity	How to Make It Lean
Gather and document the final lessons learned.	Apply yokoten to rapidly share the lessons learned during the project with appropriate people.
Document a final progress report.	Report that the Future State Value Stream Map is now in place. Document the customer value. Share the plan for continuous improvements going forward.
Celebrate Success!	

Section 5

EPILOGUE

Celebrating Success

Every NBT team member was proud of the work they had accomplished. To top it off, they received some intel that their competitor, Tornado, was still working on microprocessor technology with no completion date in sight.

Sam had previously advised Kyle to take time to celebrate successes with the team, even if it meant coordinating small celebrations that didn't require any funding. But in this case, Eamon had a little extra funding in his department's budget. He was so impressed with the outcome of the NBT project that he was happy to give Kyle some of the funding to treat the team to a celebration.

So, the following Tuesday, Kyle invited the entire team, Eamon, Sam, and even Emma to a team dinner at a local restaurant to celebrate the NBT project's success. He also had a cake decorated that had a picture of the new NBT drone on it. Above the picture, it said "Congratulations NBT Team!"

Once everyone arrived at the restaurant and made their way to the large, reserved room, Kyle addressed the group. "This has been an incredible journey and there couldn't have been a better team working on this project. I thank you all for your contributions."

Then he looked over at Sam. "I would like to especially thank Sam for teaching us all how to apply Lean Project Management." Everyone smiled and clapped their hands.

Sam smiled. "Thank you, Kyle, and thanks to all of you for your great work on this project, and for your willingness to learn about Lean Project Management. It was a great experience for me too."

As Kyle listened, his thoughts flashed back to that Terrible Tuesday. He remembered how frustrating his job was back then, and he appreciated where he was today. He had evolved into a confident project manager and a leader, thanks to Sam and the NBT project.

Eamon spoke up to share what he learned with the group. "Thanks to this team and to this project, I learned how to be a better project sponsor." As he sat down, he thought to himself, *many of our previous problems could have been avoided if I had understood how to be a good sponsor and how to apply Lean Project Management. Things will be much different going forward.*

Charles had to add his thoughts. "Speaking for the team members, we're proud to be part of a such a successful project. In the past, when we finally completed a project and launched a new product, we fearfully waited for the first customer and consumer complaints to roll in. This time, we're confident of the quality we produced. We can't wait to see the great product that we created get into the hands of consumers. We can't wait to see it flying in the air!" The rest of the team smiled in agreement.

Emma thought about the successes of both the NBT project and the final product. She walked to the front of the room to address the group. "Thank you to each and every one of you for doing your part to create and launch this new product with ground-breaking technology. I appreciate how the team met the goals for on-time delivery, cost, and performance. I feel confident there is minimal waste for us and maximum value for our customers."

She looked over at Sam and Kyle. "The project management for the NBT product has been as close to perfect as I could hope for." Everyone cheered.

As Emma made her way back to her seat, she thought about how the culture of The Flying Machine was changing for the better. *It's now a continuously improving organization based on Lean Project Management, where all team members view Lean and project management as a way of thinking and acting. Team members take pride in their work now, and unlike that Terrible Tuesday, they truly enjoy their work.*

Kyle looked over at Sam while raising his glass to offer a toast. "To the success of the NBT project – thanks to the team and to Lean Project Management!"

Then all the team members raised and clinked their glasses together. They spent the rest of their dinner sharing their experiences and talking about everything they learned. They even joked a little about the past rift between Kyle and Charles.

THE PAYBACK IS REAL

You can deliver projects faster by following a solid project management plan sprinkled with Lean principles. It sounds counterintuitive because you'll be applying more techniques and it will likely take more time up-front, but it works. The payback is real.

When your team takes on a Lean Project Management culture, you allow the right amount of time for planning, identifying, and assessing risks, getting to the root cause of problems, communicating, evaluating, and setting the stage for achieving the ideal future state.

The end result is that you'll spend significantly *less* time during the execution and closing of your projects. You'll avoid rework, putting out project fires, trying to figure out what went wrong, trying to get back on track, and placing (or avoiding) blame.

Your competitors will continue to struggle in these areas, delaying their products, and increasing their costs, while you outpace them and increase your profits.

Appendix A
Health Evaluation
for Lean Projects

To help you practice Lean Project Management, I created the following checklist called Health Evaluation for Lean Projects (HELP). Use it to help determine if your project is healthy, and ready to move forward, at each phase in the project lifecycle.

If you're a leader of project managers, or a project sponsor, these are questions you should ask the project manager. If the answer is not "yes" for most of the questions, the project may be at risk — and it's worth taking the time to go back and get those items successfully completed.

HEALTH EVALUATION FOR LEAN PROJECTS – INITIATING PHASE

Project Management Questions:

☐ Yes / ☐ No   Is it clear who the project manager and the sponsor are?

☐ Yes / ☐ No   Do the sponsor and the project manager formally agree to the charter document?

☐ Yes / ☐ No   Does the charter include a scope statement? Is it clear what's in, and not in, the project's scope?

☐ Yes / ☐ No   Is the project completion acceptance criteria measurable?

☐ Yes / ☐ No   Has the project manager been granted the authority necessary to execute the project?

Lean Questions:

☐ Yes / ☐ No   Has the voice of the customer (VOC) been formally documented?

☐ Yes / ☐ No   Have Gemba walks taken place to observe the cultural climate, existing problems, and more?

☐ Yes / ☐ No   Is it clear what standard work exists and how it can be leveraged?

☐ Yes / ☐ No   Is it clear whether/what current state value stream maps already exist?

HEALTH EVALUATION FOR LEAN PROJECTS – PLANNING PHASE

Project Management Questions:

☐ Yes / ☐ No   Was there a Project Kickoff Meeting?

☐ Yes / ☐ No   Were the project deliverables reviewed?

☐ Yes / ☐ No   Does a detailed, documented schedule exist?

☐ Yes / ☐ No   Does the schedule highlight all the major milestones?

☐ Yes / ☐ No   Did subject matter experts provide input on the schedule?

☐ Yes / ☐ No   Has the schedule been communicated to all stakeholders?

☐ Yes / ☐ No   Has a stakeholder assessment been completed and documented?

☐ Yes / ☐ No   Do you know what each key stakeholder expects, and has it been documented?

☐ Yes / ☐ No   Have you assessed the organization's willingness to accept changes that will require the people to work differently as a result of your project?

☐ Yes / ☐ No   Have you adjusted your stakeholder management plan to account for resistance to change?

☐ Yes / ☐ No   Have you documented a communication plan and shared it?

☐ Yes / ☐ No   Is there a system in place to measure and track progress?

☐ Yes / ☐ No   Has a cost estimate been documented?

☐ Yes / ☐ No   Has a scope change control process been documented?

☐ Yes / ☐ No   Have the key risks been identified, prioritized, and documented?

☐ Yes / ☐ No   Has a risk response plan been documented?

☐ Yes / ☐ No   Has risk mitigation work been factored into the project cost, schedule and scope?

☐ Yes / ☐ No   Was the team involved in the risk assessment?

☐ Yes / ☐ No   Are the sponsor and all the stakeholders aware of the high-level risks and responses?

☐ Yes / ☐ No   Is it clear which resources are needed to complete the project?

☐ Yes / ☐ No   Have the necessary resources been committed to the project?

☐ Yes / ☐ No   Have all the team members' roles and responsibilities been clearly defined, communicated, and documented?

☐ Yes / ☐ No   Have all statements of work and contracts been reviewed and approved?

Lean Questions:

☐ Yes / ☐ No   Have you practiced nemawashi to obtain

consensus/ agreement on the Project Charter and other areas of importance?

☐ Yes / ☐ No　Has an obeya room been reserved for the project?

☐ Yes / ☐ No　Do current state value stream maps highlight all the existing problem areas?

☐ Yes / ☐ No　Have you documented the root causes for all the highlighted problems?

☐ Yes / ☐ No　Have you created A3 documents to help determine the root causes of problems?

☐ Yes / ☐ No　Did you ask the Five Whys to help determine all the root causes of problems?

☐ Yes / ☐ No　Have you created future state value stream maps?

☐ Yes / ☐ No　Has the team conducted kaizen and kaikaku events to address problem areas?

☐ Yes / ☐ No　Is the team aware of (and on guard for) the Eight Forms of Waste?

☐ Yes / ☐ No　Is the team planning poka-yoke into processes, procedures, and products to avoid mistakes?

Project Management Questions:

☐ Yes / ☐ No   Are all scope change requests documented and assessed for project impacts?

☐ Yes / ☐ No   Are only approved scope changes implemented?

☐ Yes / ☐ No   When scope changes are denied, are the reasons listed in the Scope Change Log?

☐ Yes / ☐ No   Are the actual expenses tracked against the baseline cost estimate?

☐ Yes / ☐ No   Are the actual completion dates tracked against the planned schedule?

☐ Yes / ☐ No   Are issues documented in an Issue Log?

☐ Yes / ☐ No   Does the project team have access to the Issue Log?

☐ Yes / ☐ No   Is it clear who is assigned to address specific issues?

☐ Yes / ☐ No   Are there regular team meetings?

☐ Yes / ☐ No   Is the team communicating about and acting on any new risks?

☐ Yes / ☐ No   Have the team members been given constructive feedback on their performance?

☐ Yes / ☐ No   Are progress updates regularly communicated

to the sponsor and stakeholders?

Lean Questions:

☐ Yes / ☐ No   Are team huddle meetings taking place on a regular basis?

☐ Yes / ☐ No   Is the team delivering only what the customer values, and letting the customer pull what is expected?

☐ Yes / ☐ No   Are visual displays and metrics available in the obeya room and on a shared stakeholder website for all stakeholders to see?

☐ Yes / ☐ No   Is the team following-up on the actions arising from kaizen events and kaikaku events?

☐ Yes / ☐ No   Is the team meeting the objectives of the Future State Value Stream Map?

☐ Yes / ☐ No   Is the team focused on continuously improving processes, procedures, etc.?

HEALTH EVALUATION FOR LEAN PROJECTS – CLOSING PHASE

Project Management Questions:

☐ Yes / ☐ No   Has the project sponsor approved the final deliverable(s)?

☐ Yes / ☐ No   Has the customer(s) approved the final deliverable(s)?

☐ Yes / ☐ No   Have all the contracts and purchase orders been closed?

☐ Yes / ☐ No   Have all the stakeholders been notified that all work on the project has been successfully completed?

☐ Yes / ☐ No   Have the team members been released to work on other projects?

☐ Yes / ☐ No   Have the final lessons learned been documented?

☐ Yes / ☐ No   Has a final status report been compared to the Business Case goals and communicated?

Lean Questions:

☐ Yes / ☐ No   Has the team conducted a quality check?

☐ Yes / ☐ No   Has the team conducted a final review for defects?

☐ Yes / ☐ No   Have you conducted nemawashi and obtained a formal consensus/approval of the deliverable(s)?

☐ Yes / ☐ No   Is there a documented transition-to-support plan for continuously supporting, improving and aligning the product with the customer's expectations?

☐ Yes / ☐ No   Has yokoten been applied to rapidly share the lessons learned from the project?

☐ Yes / ☐ No   Is there a documented communication plan to report that the Future State Value Stream Map is now in place?

Glossary

5S – a five-step methodology used to help build an organized and uncluttered work environment: sort, set in order, shine, systematize, standardize

Black Belt – a person with a Six Sigma black belt certification who leads problem-solving projects, trains, and coaches project teams by following the DMAIC model

closing – the fifth and final phase of the project lifecycle in which the final deliverables are accepted and more

communication management – the collection, creation, storage, monitoring, and distribution, of project information

contingency plan – a reactive risk response that is used if, and only if, a specific risk turns into a reality

contract – a formal legal agreement involving the exchange of goods or services

cost management – estimating the initial cost of a project and then managing any cost variances that occur during the life of a project

critical path – the path of the longest task durations in the project defects – a type of deficiency or error within a project or product

deliverable – the measurable goods or services provided upon the completion of a project or product.

DMAIC – Define, Measure, Analyze, Improve, and Control is an improvement tool with five process steps used to drive Six Sigma projects

DOWNTIME – acronym for the eight forms of waste (defects, overproduction, waiting, non-utilized talent, transportation, inventory, motion, excess processing)

Eight Forms of Waste – defects, overproduction, waiting, non-utilized talent, transportation, inventory, motion, excess processing

excess processing – doing more work than is necessary; addressing problems without understanding the root causes

executing – the third phase of the project lifecycle when work is performed according to the plan (and more)

flow – smooth movement through a project or process generated by eliminating opportunities for waste to enter or re-enter a process

Gantt chart – a type of horizontal bar chart used to show a project schedule, where each activity in the schedule is represented by its own horizontal bar

Gemba walk – going to an actual place where work is happening, and respectfully observing the processes taking place and the people doing their work, to gather facts for problem-solving and improving processes

gold plating – providing features the customer does not require

Green Belt a person with a Six Sigma green belt certification who assists with data collection, analysis, and problem-solving

Health Evaluation for Lean Projects (HELP) – a series of check-lists created by L.T. Harland, PMP to evaluate a project's health during every phase of a project's lifecycle

high-level – goals or plans described in general, rather than in detail

huddle – a brief meeting usually held at the start of each day to set a team's direction

initiating – the first phase of the project lifecycle where a project manager is selected, a charter is created and more

integration management – necessary management, balancing and prioritization of work when some or all the project knowledge areas are happening simultaneously or overlapping

inventory – excess materials, work in process, or finished goods

issue – an event or situation that has occurred and has negative consequences for a project

Just in Time (JIT) – a type of inventory management in which the materials, labor and other needed items are scheduled to arrive at the precise time they are needed

kaikaku – a Japanese term meaning radical change

kaizen – a Japanese term meaning incremental change

Kickoff Meeting – the first formal meeting held by the project manager to review the project charter and more

Lean project management – a combination of Lean and project management that enables the meeting of delivery, cost and performance goals while reducing waste and focusing on customer value

lessons learned – experiences gained from a project that are gathered and documented to be used as a reference for future projects

mitigation plan – a documented, proactive risk response strategy to reduce the probability a risk will happen, or the impact of a risk

monitoring and controlling – overseeing of a project's tasks and metrics to ensure it stays within scope, on time, and on budget

motion – any wasted motion to move parts or people

muda – wastefulness

mura – unevenness, irregularity

muri – overburden, excessiveness

nemawashi – a Japanese term for an informal process of gaining consensus

non-utilized talent – the result when you have poor assignment and communication of roles and responsibilities

obeya room – a room dedicated to a specific project, used to share knowledge, and to optimize communication and transparency

organizational Structure – how a company is organized for managing projects

over Production – producing more than is needed or producing something before it is needed

plan-do-check-act (PDCA) – the Lean operating framework and a methodology used for implementing kaizen and kaikaku events

perfection – the endless pursuit of improving processes until the perfect conditions are reached

planning – the second phase of the project lifecycle, during which detailed work is planned, communications are planned, risks are assessed, and more

PM Trailblazer, LLC – an organization that provides Lean Project Management consulting, many different types of customized training, a Health Evaluation for Lean Projects (HELP), and free project management templates to help you manage your Lean projects. Visit www.PMtrailblazer.com

poka-yoke – mistake-proofing or taking all possible measures to prevent mistakes from happening portfolio – a group of related programs that are typically grouped together for a business reason

procurement management – the creation of relationships with outside suppliers for goods or services that are needed for a project

product development process – a formal process followed to take a product idea from concept to commercialization

program – a group of related projects

project – any planned undertaking that is meant to achieve a goal

project charter – a formal document describing the high-level goals of a project, what a project will deliver, when it will be delivered, the allowable cost, and who the key stakeholders are. It is created during the Initiating Phase of a project and should be formally approved by the project sponsor before the project planning begins.

project lifecycle – a model for managing projects that includes five phases: initiating, planning, executing, monitoring and controlling, and closing

project management – planning and executing projects to meet their intended cost, schedule and quality objectives

project management waste – waste occurring in projects, often impacting cost, schedules and customer value

project manager – the person who leads the planning and execution of a project, as well as the team

pull – a Lean term for only delivering value that a customer has requested and when they request it

purchase order – a formal document issued by a buyer to a seller indicating the type, quantity, and an agreed upon price for products or services

quality – the degree to which a project fulfills its requirements

quality assurance – building in quality early in a process

quality control – inspecting for defects later in a process

RACI – a chart that outlines activities assigned to people or roles, indicating who is Responsible, Accountable, Consulted and Informed.

release (or request) for proposal (RFP)- the solicitation of a proposal to solve a particular need or problem, often made through a bidding process by a company/government interested in buying/procuring a product or service. An RFP is sent to potential sellers to submit their business proposals

release for quotation (RFQ) – same as release (or request) for proposal, but used after a particular need or problem has been resolved to solicit a proposal

resource management – determining which resources are needed throughout the life of a project, hiring, developing, retaining, and motivating people

risk – an event that may or may not occur, but if it does happen it could negatively impact a project risk assessment – ranking risks to show their levels of impact and probability

risk identification – listing the risks that could occur throughout the life of a project

risk management – the identification, assessment, and mitigation of project risks

risk response – a strategy to address the risks identified and reduce their impact and probability of happening

root cause – the earliest or initial cause of a situation

schedule management – estimating the time it will take to complete a project, and then managing any schedule variances that occur during the life of the project

scope creep – when uncontrolled changes occur within a project after the project's charter has been approved

scope management – defining all the work required to complete a project, making sure that all of it (and only it) is completed, and following a scope change control process

sensei – a teacher of Lean principles who guides a team through the journey of applying Lean

Six Sigma – a level of quality with a maximum of 3.4 defective parts per million (PPM) products or processes delivered

statement of work (SOW) – a formal description of a project's work that defines deliverables and timelines for a supplier who provides services to a client

sponsor – person who selects a project manager to lead a project, provides funding for the project, agrees to the deliverables documented in the charter, agrees on the final acceptance criteria, and ultimately signs off on the completed deliverables

stakeholder – a person or an organization who is impacted by a project, either positively or negatively

stakeholder management – identifying all the stakeholders and keeping them satisfied, engaged, and informed throughout the life of a project

standard work – created to enable different people to perform 'repeat' tasks in the same way

status update – tracking and reporting the progress of a project during a point in time

Terrible Tuesday – the day that a project The Flying Machine team had been dedicating their time to for over a year was canceled due to poor project management

the Five Whys – a simple method for finding the root cause of a problem by asking a sequence of "Why?" questions five or more times

transportation waste – wasted effort transporting items

triple constraint – also referred to as the project management triangle, the sides or points of the triangle represent scope, time, and cost.

value – a good or service which meets a customer's needs at a specific price at a specific time, and the end result when waste is removed

value added – For an activity to be considered value added, a customer must be willing to pay for it, it must transform a project/product/service toward completion, and it must be done correctly the first time

value stream – all the value added, as well as any non-value-added steps, necessary to take a product or service from its conception all the way to completion, including its use by the end customer

visual management boards – provide information graphically, such as status reports and more, that can be viewed at a glance

visual control – using signs, graphics, or other forms of eye-catching displays instead of written instructions to standardize, improve efficiency, and enhance clarity

visual management methods – simple graphic tools used to quickly show the current status to anyone within a minute

voice of the customer – documentation of the customer's perspective, needs, expectations, preferences, and comments

waiting – one of the eight forms of waste that includes waiting for project work to begin, waiting for approvals, supplies, etc.

waste – non-value-added activity

work breakdown structure – a decomposition or a visual breakdown of a project into smaller components yokoten – a rapid sharing of best practices across an organization

Index

Recommended Reading

Brewer, Jeffrey L. and Dittman, Kevin C. *Methods of IT Project Management.* Pearson Education, Inc., 2013

Sayer, Natalie J. and Williams, Bruce. *Lean for Dummies.* John Wiley and Sons, Inc., 2012

Morgan, James M. and Liker, Jeffrey K. *The Toyota Product Development System.* Productivity Press, 2006

Carter, Lynda. *The Practitioner's Guide to Project Management: Simple, Effective Techniques That Deliver Business Value.* Competitive Edge Consulting, Inc., 2014

Gilpatrick, Keith and Furlong, Brian. *The Elusive Lean Enterprise: Why Companies Struggle to get the Full Benefits from Lean.* Multi-Media Publications, Inc., 2007

Shook, John. Managing to Learn. Using the A3 *Managing Process to Solve Problems, Gain Agreement, Mentor, and Lead.* Lean Enterprise Institute, Inc., 2008

Mulcahy, Rita PMP, et al. *Rita Mulcahy's PMP Exam Prep.* RMC Publications, Inc., 2018

Womack, James P. and Jones, Daniel T. *Lean Thinking. Banish Waste and Create Wealth in Your Organization.* Free Press, 2003

Frankel, Lois P. PhD. *Nice Girls Don't Get the Corner Office: Unconscious Mistakes Women Make That Sabotage Their Careers.* Business Plus, 2014

Scott, Susan. *Fierce Conversations: Achieving Success at Work and Life, One Conversation at a Time.* Berkley, 2004

Sandberg, Sheryl with Scovell, Nell. *Lean In: Women, Work, and the Will to Lead.* Knopf, 2013.

WEBSITES, BLOGS AND SOCIAL MEDIA

PMtrailblazer.com

PMI.org

Lean.org

LeanBlog.org

ASQ.org

Join on Facebook:
Ninja Project Manager